RESEARCH METHODOLOGY IN SOCIAL SCIENCES

By the Same Author

- Financial Services in India
- Financial Markets and Institutions
- Portfolio Management

About the Author

Dr. G. Ramesh Babu, Lecturer in Commerce, S.S.R. Jyothi College, Khammam, has vast teaching experience of 18 years at U.G. and P.G. levels. Academically, he is Ph.D. in Industrial Finance. He has published many papers in various management and commerce journals of repute and has also presented papers in various conferences. He is an active member of the All India Management Association, New Delhi; Associate Member of Society for Capital Market and Research, New Delhi; and Associate Member of Indian Institute of Public Administration, New Delhi. His areas of interest include Financial Systems and Capital Market.

RESEARCH METHODOLOGY
in
SOCIAL SCIENCES

(For M.Phil, MSW, MBA, Pre-Ph.D and Post-doctoral courses)

Dr. G. Ramesh Babu
M. Com. Ph.D., MIAM,
Asst. Professor in Commerce
SSRJ Arts and Science College
Khammam-507003, A.P.
E-mail : gurda_rameshbabu.yahoo mail.com

CONCEPT PUBLISHING COMPANY, NEW DELHI-110059

Cataloging in Publication Data--DK
Courtesy: D.K. Agencies (P) Ltd. <docinfo@dkagencies.com>

Ramesh Babu, G. (Gunda), 1963-
Research methodology in social sciences / G. Ramesh Babu.
p. cm.
Includes bibliographical references.
Includes index.
ISBN 13: 9788180695384
ISBN 8180695395

1. Social sciences--Research--Methodology-Textbooks. I. Title.

DDC 300.723 22

ISBN-13: 978-81-8069-538-4 (HB)
ISBN-10: 81-8069-538-7 (HB)

First Published 2008

Published and Printed by
Ashok Kumar Mittal
Concept Publishing Company
A/15-16, Commercial Block, Mohan Garden
New Delhi-110059 (INDIA)

Phones : 25351460, 25351794
Fax : 091-11-25357103
Email : publishing@conceptpub.com

PREFACE

Research is a subject of growing importance in the digital era. It is based on knowledge. Research means "Re-search for information". The ability to conduct research in an area requires in-depth knowledge in that area and the experience of working on research problems. Ability to identify research problems is one of the important characters of a good researcher. Research requires a good knowledge of recent developments in the respective field. It must involve innovation and creation of interest. Research results should be useful to society. The fruits of the research or experiment may enhance the living standards of the layman. In this book an attempt is made to give a comprehensive coverage of research aspects in social sciences. This book has been written as per the syllabus prescribed for the M.Phil in Social Sciences, Pre-Ph.D., Post-doctoral, MSW, MA (Personnel Management) and MBA. I am confident that this book will help the students and faculty members of social sciences.

Since the book is a synthesis, I am indebted to all authors who have contributed to the research aspects in social sciences. It is my pleasure to make acknowledgements of every idea whose sources have been identified. I am indebted to my colleagues both academic and professionals, and countless students. It would be impossible to list them all. For evincing personal interest in understanding a project of this magnitude and making invaluable suggestions from time to time, it is my duty to express grateful thanks to Late Shri K. Ram Mohan, President, Jyothi Education Society, who inspired me always to work in an uncompromising environment in the field of education. Shri P. Raghurama Rao, Treasurer, Jyothi Education Society, is a motivational factor behind every project taken up by me. Dr. D. Ramachandra Bose, Principal, S.S.R. Jyothi College is always an inspirational factor behind talent in the family of Jyothi Education Society. I must also place on record my sincere thanks to my teachers Shri K.V. Kameswar Rao, Shri P.V. Anjaneyulu and G. Satyanarayana. I am also thankful to Dr. K. Srinivasa Rao for giving valuable suggestions.

I owe my gratitude to Shri Ashok Kumar Mittal of Concept Publishing Company for giving his personal attention in expediting printing of the book.

I would like to extend and my sincere thanks to Dr. P. Madhusudan Rao, Professor of Commerce and Business Management, University Post Graduate College, Khammam for his valuable guidance in completion of this book.

Dr. G. Ramesh Babu

CONTENTS

Preface v

UNIT I

1. Research Methodology 3

UNIT II
DESIGNING OF RESEARCH PROPOSAL

1. Research Design 41
2. Sampling Design 57
3. Scaling Techniques 72
4. Collection of Data 95
5. Analysis of Data 120
6. Fundamentals of Sampling 138
7. Testing of Hypothesis (Parametric and Non-Parametric) 156

Index 213

UNIT I

1

RESEARCH METHODOLOGY

Introduction

The universe contains unknown facts. Man should be educated through a learning process. The process provides many known facts to the learner. The universe is a reflection of number of various kinds of elements. The man is searching for unknown facts. The searching process is known as "Research". Research means, search for knowledge. It is a systematic search for a specific topic. It is an art of investigation. Investigation consists of a series of consequences of facts finding. It is an art of scientific investigation. It is an academic activity. It stimulates the abilities of a learner. It enhances the knowledge of a person. Knowledge is a powerful weapon to counter poverty. Knowledge is based on acquired information. Information is the most important factor in gaining knowledge. The knowledge of a person can be determined on the basis of acquired information. Hence the term research has been defined by various persons according to their perception.

"A careful investigation or enquiry specially through search for new facts in any branch of knowledge."

—Advanced Learners Dictionary.[1]

"The manipulation of things, concepts or symbols for the purpose of generalising to extend, correct or verify knowledge whether that knowledge aids in construction of theory or in the practice of an art"

—D. Slesinger and M. Stephenson.[2]

"Systematised effort to gain new knowledge."

—Redman and Mory.[3]

"Research comprises defining and redefining problems, formulating hypothesis or suggested solutions; collecting, organising and evaluating data, making deductions and reaching conclusions and at last carefully testing the conclusions to determine whether they fit the formulating hypothesis." —Clifford Woody

Research is an art of scientific investigation. It is a voyage of discovery. It is involved with innovation and creativity. It is useful to probe about unknown things. It helps us to attain full understanding of the unexposed things. The hidden things will be exposed to the universe by the research only. Research is the expansion of original knowledge and requires a continuous monitoring. It shows the way for advancement of knowledge regarding a specific topic. Fact is to be exposed with the help of scientific study, in-depth observation, comparison and experiment. It provides a solution to a problem. It also helps in generalisation and formulations of new theories and inventions. It refers to study the scientific observation regarding a problem. It involves collection of data, analysis of data, framing hypothesis, finding conclusions, etc. to reach the goal of researcher. It is one of the tools in the hands of a social scientist. It is useful to make inquiry about a specific task or problems.

Objectives of Research

Research is to find solution through application of scientific approach. The purpose of conducting a research is to find out the truth. The truth has been a hidden fact which is unexposed. Every research study has its own specific purpose usually research objectives can be categorised as follows:

(a) Universe is a reflection of new things at every movement. Research provides a way to discover new things in every movement of time. Research facilitates achieving new insights.
(b) Research creates an opportunity to study the characteristics of a particular individual or situation or a group.
(c) Research facilitates study about the problem which arises frequently.

The basic objective of research is to study the relationship between two variables. The relation between two factors can be tested through **"Hypothesis"**.

Research is a reflection of many new things surrounded by us. It discovers new facts from our universe. The research can be further classified as **"exploratory research studies, descriptive research studies, diagnostic research studies, hypothesis testing research studies"**. All about these research studies can be studied in preceding pages at the reference of context. Research can be to explore new things, new solutions, new insights regarding a particular phenomenon. It involves gathering knowledge about a specific area of specialisation.

The research will be carried out by a research scholar for the purpose of getting a research degree (Ph.D.). It can be used as a weapon, desire to face the challenge in the unsolved problem. A lot of problems faced by the society initiates a scholar to take up a research theme. It will be carried out by research scholars because of a desire for intellectual satisfaction for creative work. It provides benefits to the society. Any research conducted by anyone is meant for the use of society. Some other research initiatives are taken by the directives of government organisations, non-government organisations, business organisations and scientific research organisations. **For ex:** University Grants Commission sponsors research programmes on various subjects. **Indian Council of Social Science Research** conducts research programmes in social sciences. **National Council of Applied Economic Research** sponsors the research programmes in the area of specialisation of **Econometrics. Indian Statistical Institute** conducts research surveys regarding savings habits of the country. **Indian Council of Agricultural Research** is involved in conducting research programmes in agriculture sector. **Indian Institute of Science** has focused mainly on scientific applications of aerospace engineering sector. **Council of Scientific and Industrial Research** is fully involved in industrial research applications. Strong research and development organisations are necessary for the development of our nation. A number of other factor such as social thinking, curiosity about new happenings, economic conditions, moral value of the society, cultural revolution factors forced scholars to perform research operations in various fields of subjects of interest.

Types of Research Programmes

Research is useful to change the human lifestyle. It is an innovative and intellectual activity. It is a fact-finding tool. Any research programme carried out by any researcher is targeted to the benefits of the community. Generally there are various kinds of research programmes extent in the country which are presented below for a detailed discussions.

(A) Descriptive and Analytical Research study
(B) Quantitative and Qualitative Research study
(C) Applied and Fundamental Research study
(D) Empirical and Conceptual Research study
(E) Miscellaneous Research study

(A) Descriptive and Analytical Research Study

Descriptive research studies about the description of the state of affairs that exists at present. The study may also be undertaken in the field of business and industry. It includes surveys and fact-finding enquiries. In this study, the researcher has to report what is happening regarding a particular aspect. He has no control over the aspects of the study. He has to report only a current situation regarding a particular phenomenon. His duty is to report the current situation only. He has a limited role to play in his assignment. The descriptive research is useful to commercial enterprises to know about the consumer behaviour. **For ex:** buying pattern of consumers, frequency of shopping, buying decisions, etc. The research study discovers the courses in business sector. The study includes all kinds of survey methods including comparative and correlation methods. **Analytical research study** is based on facts. It has to use facts and analyse the situation. The researcher has to conduct the research based on available information. The researcher has to make a typical evaluation of material. It is based on available facts only.

(B) Quantitative and Qualitative Research Study

Quantitative research is another kind of research study. It is based on the terms of quantity. It indicates the measurement of quantity. It deals with the analysis of numericals. It reflects the scientific analysis of data. The study indicates the fluctuations regarding performance of a business concern, or any organisation in terms of measurement of quantity or data. In this method the data will be analysed on the basis of some characteristics. **For ex:** Height, weight, income, sales, profit, production. **Qualitative research** is associated with qualitative phenomenon. It reveals the quality aspects of a particular phenomenon. It is related to psychological aspects of human behaviour. It is one of the methods to find out the feelings of the public. It is meant to know the opinion or attitude of the public. The research programme is designed to know the feelings of the public regarding a particular phenomenon. It may be conducted about a particular institution or subject. It is useful to discover the underlying motives of human behaviour which cannot be explored in other ways. This kind of research studies explores the psychological aspects of human behaviour at various times in a situation. It describes the characterisation of a particular thing. It does not analyse data based observation. It takes help and guidance from **psychologists. It is useful** in conducting **in-depth** interviews. It is also known as **"motivation research"**. Motivation research brings out inner feelings of the motives and desires of a human being. Qualitative research uses other techniques such as **word association tests, sentence completion tests, story competition tests**, etc. Another popular method **"opinion research"** is conducted at the time of general elections in order to know the pulse of the voters. They are popularly known as **"exit polls"**. This research is conducted to determine how the people will react to the political parties' manifestos. The qualitative research is a difficult task. Therefore, the researcher should pay adequate attention to the task before carrying out a research assignment.

(C) Applied and Fundamental Research Study

Applied research has a wider base of applications. It is reflected in all walks of life of a layman. It is related to economic, social and political aspects of the country. It has a broad base of applications. It aims at finding a solution for an immediate problem facing by a **society or a nation or a business organisation**. It provides immediate solution to the problems facing the nation or an organisation. **For ex:** Marketing research conducted by a commercial enterprises to know the pulse of consumer. **Fundamental Research** is also called **"Basic research"**. Fundamental research is related to formulations of theory. It is concerned with generalisations of nature. **For ex:** Research in pure mathematics, research in natural science phenomenon. **Fundamental research** also studies human behaviour at different situations. It is aimed at certain solutions facing a strong social or community problem. Applied research is action oriented, whereas fundamental research is related to finding out business solutions and economic aspects of the nation.

(D) Empirical and Conceptual Research Study

Empirical research is data based research. It is based on experience or observation in a particular aspect. It provides solutions with a strong verification of observation or experiment. It is a powerful tool to analyse the problem. It can also be called as **"experimental type of research"**. Empirical research is based on first hand information. The desired result will be arrived at through empirical analysis. It is based on guesswork. The guesswork will be tested with the hypothesis. The hypothesis can prove a positive or negative result. Evidence will be gathered through experiments. On the other hand **conceptual research** is related to developing new concepts or innovation. It is associated with interpretation of new ideas for existing method. It is usually adopted by philosophers. It is related to policy matters and associated with policy thinkers to develop new and innovative things.

(E) Miscellaneous Research Study

There are various kinds of research studies exists and are variations of one or more of the above methods. They are based on either purpose of the research or an observation of a situation at a particular time and place. All research studies are not similar and differ from various studies of research. Research can be further classified as **one time research and longitudinal research**. One time research is conducted during a single time period. It is meant for a time bound assignment. It is conducted for a specific period of time. **Longitudinal research** is conducted several times. This kind of research can be carried out over several time periods. Research can also be further classified as **conclusion oriented and decision oriented**.

Conclusion oriented research method provides full freedom to the researcher. The researcher has liberty in picking up a problem and redesigns the enquiry method. He procures the information according to his wish and conceptualise the study. **Decision oriented research** is also known as **operations research**. It is a scientific method of study to approach a problem. It is always useful for decision makers in the organisation. In this method, the researcher has no freedom to carry out the programme as per his wishes. It provides solutions to executive departments with a quantitative analysis. Research can also be classified or **"field setting research, laboratory research and simulation research"**. The research can be carried out by the researcher as per the surrounding environment. The research study follows case study methods or in-depth analysis to reach the basic normal relations. These studies are useful to probe the things in-depth as information gathering devices. The research can be further categorised as **exploratory and historical research. Exploratory research** is associated with the development of hypothesis. **Historical research** is involved with studying the past. It utilises the historical sources of information such as documents. It is associated with the study of past events or ideas of the past. It also includes the study of the philosophy of persons and groups at any period of time. The study of research depends upon many factors. Research is an innovative activity. It is an intellectual process. It provides more benefits to the community. It is an exploratory tool to get the hidden facts underlying the universe. Man is an intellectual insect. He is always interested in facts hidden in the universe.

Research Approaches

Research brings to light the fact from unknown place to known place. It is an intellectual property to the human resources. It is a continuous scientific activity. It focuses on problems to provide solution for smooth functioning of life of the human being. It facilitates a sophisticated life style to the layman. Usually research may be related to the **life sciences and social sciences**. Research in life sciences can influence the life style of a layman. A continuous research enables the society to enjoy the **cellular services**. Research in medical field provided a longer life span to the human being. A research in agriculture sector provide better yield with lower levels of rainfall or water resources. A continuous research on **"internet"** enables the layman to pay in **"online"**. A lot of legwork has been reduced to the layman. Before **IT** revolutions, everything is **"inline"** after IT revolution everything is **"online"**. Online system has made drastic changes in the lifestyle of a layman. Any research activity should be useful to the community. It should explore things that will change the life style of a layman. Basically research will bring the fact from unknown to known facts. It explores new avenues, new methods, new techniques, new inventions, all of the things meant for layman. Research in social science can also change the life style of a layman. Research in political matters reveal that, some benefits are available to the layman. **For ex: privatisation** policy enables the layman to fly in private airlines. Private flights are becoming as fragment as a **city bus services** between cities. The **open sky policy** provided an opportunity to the middle class employees to travel in flights rather than in trains. The layman life style has also been changed due to privatisation of the **telecommunication sector**. Once upon a time, telephone was a luxury product for even the rich community. But at present **mobile** is become necessary for even an illiterate person. In India, there are **16 crores** of mobile subscribers. All of these things are available to a layman on the basis of research. Hence research in social and life sciences has drastically changed the life style of the layman. However, there are two basic approaches in research i.e., **quantitative and qualitative approach**. **Quantitative approach** deals with the comparison of data. It measures the efficiency in terms of quantity. It is based on quantitative analysis. The quantitative analysis is dependent upon digital information. Data contains numerical information regarding a particular aspect. The quantitative research approach can be further divided **inferential, experimental and simulation approach**. The inferential research approach is associated with procurement of data. The researcher in this method can draw inferences from the vast data available. Data is a reservoir of numerical information. Numerical information can express a lot regarding a particular aspect. The researcher has to draw conclusions from the available data. Inferential study is related to characteristics or relationships of population. It is usually made with a survey. A survey is a tool to study the characteristics of the population. Questions are asked to draw inferences from the population. The desired information is procured and probed from the target audience through a survey method. **Experimental approach** is one method of quantitative approach. In this method, the researcher has control over the research environment. The variables are manipulated to observe their effect on other variables. The researcher has to observe how all these variable impact on each other. It is a rigid analysis. **Simulation approach** is associated with the artificial environment. The relevant data and information can be generated from this approach. It is a observation of dynamic behaviour under controlled situation. Simulation refers to an artificial environment related to operation of a numerical model that indicates the structure. It is useful in business sector. It helps to estimate future sales models of commercial enterprises. It is useful in building models for understanding future course of business.

Qualitative approach is associated with the observation of feelings, attitudes and beliefs of the public. It is related to inner feeling of the human being and to characterisation of a particular task or topic. The researcher must have insight and impressions regarding a particular topic or area of interest. **For ex:** group interviews, in-depth interviews are the best examples for qualitative approach.

Importance of Research

The research is gaining momentum slowly. It cannot be ignored. It is the basis for development of a nation. Research in all disciplines enhances the wealth of a nation. Today's progress is based on yesterday's research. Continuous research in any field provides fruitful aspects for the future. Inquiry is the basic characteristic for research. Inquiry leads to innovation. Innovation is the value addition of research. It promotes the development of logical thinking habits of a human being or an organisation. The role of research cannot be ignored in the **digital economy**. It is gaining more importance in business, applied economy and in social sciences. Research in applied economy is a greatly influential factor in government policies. A lot of rules and guidelines are framed by the government in keeping with research in applied economics. The government is using research in solving operational problems. The importance of research cannot be ignored in layman's life. The research is more useful in the following ways:

(a) Business Sector
(b) Government Sector
(c) Social Science Sector

(a) Business Sector

Research is useful for business sector. Every invention should be brought to the market. Any new product or any new service that exists in the market is the brain child of research. The market is a combination of new and old products. Market is a dynamic place. It always requires new goods and services. It is useful in business for taking decisions. In business, the research further can be grouped as **operations research, market research, and motivational research**. Operations research is useful in cost reduction programmes of the corporate sector. It can be applied for profit maximisation of the business concern. It is useful in optimum utilisation of company resources. It is related to the application of mathematical, logical and analytical techniques to the solutions of business problems. It aims at cost minimisation of the product. In a competitive world, the customer always desires at lower prices and higher quality of goods. Hence the companies are always to reach the consumers desires. In this process, the operation research is more useful to the business sector. **Market research** is another most important factor in the corporate world. No business unit can ignore the importance of market research. Market research is related to the investigation about the market structure. Market is a combination of different desires and dreams of the customers. The goods manufactured by the corporate sector will be dumped in the market for selling. For selling the goods in the market, the corporate sector should know the pulse of the customer. The goods and services are delivered by the corporate sector as per the desires and dreams of the customers. **Motivational research** is related to psychological behaviour of the market. Market is a combination of desires and dreams of the millions of the customers. It is concerned with determination of consumer behaviour. **Consumer pulse** is the most important factor for predicting the market. The market assessment will be done on the basis of consumer tastes. All these factors are greatly helpful for making business decisions. The assessment of demand factor is more useful in business environment. The corporate sector will adjust its supply and demand factors as per the market situation. **Market analysis** occupies a dominant role in determining the supply-demand adjustment for a commercial enterprises. **Sales forecasting and business budgeting** are the main ingredients in profit maximisation of the company. Sales forecasting occupies a crucial role in determining the profitability of the company. Research provides a strong decision support for making business decisions.

(b) Government Sector

Government is an official machinery to run the administration. Administration facilitates the smooth functioning of the various organs of the government. Government is one of the organ in the democratic system. It is run by a political party which act as per its manifesto. As per the manifesto promised to the voters by the political party, it fulfils the desires and dreams of the crores of public. Government policies are framed in keeping with the view of the welfare of the citizens. For implementation of government policies, it needs a large amount of financial resources. The financial resources are supplied to the government by way of presentation of budget in the Parliament. The future of the country determined by its budget. Budget is a document of consisting income and expenditure of a government. Budget will be prepared by the Government as per the needs and desires of the people. The welfare programmes of the nation, should be provided by the Government. The required financial resources are mobilised by the government through **direct and indirect taxation system**. The spending crores of rupees of the money should be utilised in a proper way. The cost of needs of the public should be equated to probable revenue to meet the desires. This is a situation, where research is needed. Research can be used as a device for the proper allocation and utilisation of financial resources. The decisions will be taken as the basis of finding of research results. Therefore, decisions may not be a part of research, but research influence the decisions of the policy makers. Research is a tool for useful to the policy makers. Government decisions are mostly influencing the lives of public directly or indirectly. The government should look after all the sections of the community such as cultivators, industry, service sectors of the whole country. Thus research is necessary for the government in solving the problems of the above sectors. Research is also useful to the government in collection of information regarding economic and social structure of the nation. The vast information collected regarding the economic situation of the nation, enables the government, what is happening in the economy and what changes are occurring in the business environment. This situation facilitates the government, to move according to the latest trends occurred in the society. Collecting statistical data, compiling information, making analysis and interpreting views of the experts are the part of research work.

(c) Social Science Sector

Research is an intellectual activity. It provides an intellectual satisfaction to the researcher. It is a knowledge-based activity. Research means knowing the unknown facts from the universe. Knowledge will be acquired through research. Research is a value addition to the existing knowledge and skills. Social scientist will apply all research techniques for the welfare of the society. His knowledge will be utilised for the purpose of gaining benefit to the society. Social science clearly knows the movement and behaviour of a human being. It has practical ability to do something better or in a more efficient manner for the welfare of the society. Its role is increasing in solving immediate problems of human relations. In addition to the above, the significance of research can also be observed keeping in view the following points:

- (i) The research scholars, those who are pursuing Ph.D., thesis, they can attain high position in the society.
- (ii) The policy makers and philosophers can use research as a guiding force for new ideas and innovative things.
- (iii) Intellectuals and experts may use research for formation of new theories and generalisations.
- (iv) Research professionals like social scientists, research officers, research assistants may choose research as their career.
- (v) Research may develop new styles and creative work in pursuing of professional work of men and women in the society.

Research is a reservoir of knowledge and useful in solving different kinds of problems in business, governmental and social problems. It is a formal training to understand the intricacies of the various problems exist in society.

Research Methodology

Research means knowing unknown facts from the universe. In the process of knowing facts, the researcher should have taken this assignment in a systematic and in a proper way. The systematic way of doing research is known as **"Research Methodology"**. The scientific way of pursuing research is also called as research methodology. It enables the development of indices and statistical tools to be used in research projects. Researcher should be thorough in application of statistical techniques like mean, mode, median, standard deviations and chi-square etc. The researcher should also know about these techniques, how far these tools are relevant to the research problem. He should know the intricacies of various techniques of applicability of statistical tools as per the research project requirement. He should design the research project with appropriate tools to be used in his project. The research projects are different from problem to problem. The research projects designed by the social scientist will be evaluated by another researcher. The research methodology has many dimensions.

Research Methods

Research means knowing facts from unknown things in the universe. The unknown fact will be known by the researcher through a process is known as **Research Method**. Research method can be used for smooth functioning and completion of a project. Research methods are part of the analytical tools of research. It refers to the behaviour and instruments used in selecting and constructing research technique. The library research, field research, and laboratory research constitutes various kinds of study of a research problem. **Library research process** deals with the analysis of evidences such as historical records and documents. **Field research** constitutes a number of research methods to solve the existing research problems such as **"case study group interview, mass observation, personal interview, focused interview, participant observations etc."**. **Laboratory research** contains the methods such as role play, role analysis, study of small group behaviour etc. Research methods can be used by the researcher in performing research operations. A researcher who uses methods during the course studying his research problems are known as **Research Methods**. Research methods can be put into three groups, **collection of data, statistical techniques, evaluation of results**.

Scientific Method

Science is related to achieve a systematic interrelation of facts. It relies on empirical evidence. It is object oriented. It is logical and systematic method. It is free from personal bias or prejudice. Scientific method is the pursuit of truth as determined by logical considerations. Scientific method is based on logic and it predicts accurately. Logic develops a number of series of consequences. The consequences will be compared with observable factors. Scientific method includes experimentation and survey investigations. Experiments are necessary to solve a problem. It is done to test hypothesis and discover new relationship. Sometimes experiments may either poorly designed or faulty assumptions contains or badly executed experiments. Investigations may also provides information for drawing inferences. Scientific method enable to verify qualities of phenomenon related to research problems. A researcher is always guided by the rules of logical reasoning. Research and scientific methods are closely related. Research is an inquiry for knowing unknown facts from the universe. Scientific methods are part of research.

Research Process

Research means **re-search** for unknown fact. Research methodology provides a better training facility in gathering information, collection of data, arranging in a chronological way, participating in the field-work, use of statistical tools, designing questionnaires, recording evidences, etc. Inferences from the experiments and collected data will require skill of the researcher. The importance of research methodology is presented below for further understanding of the concept.

(a) Research methodology enables the researcher to do his research work more confidently.
(b) Research methodology cultivate the abilities of the researcher.
(c) Research methodology will pull out the hidden talent of the researcher.
(d) Research methodology will be more useful in finding the **pulse** of consumers.

The adoption of research tools, statistical techniques enables the process of research more easily. Research process contains a number of series of actions necessary for the smooth completion of research work without any hurdles. Research process consists of the following steps to carry out the research project without any problems:

(a) Statement of the research problems
(b) Review of literature
(c) Framing the hypothesis
(d) Research design
(e) Selection of samples
(f) Collection of data
(g) Implementation of project work
(h) Analysis of data
(i) Testing of hypothesis
(j) Interpretations
(k) Conclusions and suggestions

(a) Statement of the Research Problems

The researcher should find out the research problem which he wants to study. Problem identification is the most important factor in taking up of a research task. Research means, a scientific study of inquiry regarding a specific task. Usually there are two kinds of research problems exists in the universe: (a) related to nature, (b) related to **two variables**. The researcher should decide himself about the study. The researcher may decide the general area of interest or related to subject matter that he would like to investigate. The researcher interest and intention is the most important factor in framing the research problem. The researcher should be able to understand and the problem thoroughly. A clear understanding of the problem enables the researcher to reach his destination more easily and in a sophisticated way. He can reduce the time and expenses, if he would have experticism in the subject matter. For a **doctoral thesis work**, the research guide always provides help to his research scholar. Generally, the research guide will be at the level of **Professor**, who is an expert and **reservoir** of knowledge in that subject matter. He may immediately react to the researcher's problems and provides his best experticism to reach the destination. The research guide is a person, who involved in various research projects and acquired more efficiency in solving the problem. The research work in non-academic areas such as in private business units or in government organisations, the work is earmarked by the administrative organs. The researcher can discuss the problem with the concerned officials and involve in its solving problem. The researcher should also be equipped with the available literature to get solutions more easily. Review of literature enables the student or researcher to understand the problem more easily.

(b) Review of Literature

The researcher's next important task is to gather all the information about the past research work undertaken by various scholars. The review of literature can be classified in two kinds: (a) review regarding conceptual literature, (b) review in empirical literature. The review regarding these two aspects will generate an idea in the mind of researcher. Therefore, the researcher can make his work very smoothly and sophisticatedly. After identification of the problem, a brief summary should be prepared and written down. The research scholar should write a **synopsis** regarding his topic and submit it to the research board through research guide for approval. In this situation, while preparing the synopsis, the research scholar should gather extensive literature survey regarding his research problem. For an in-depth collection of information, he has to refer research journals, books, magazines, published bibliographies, unpublished working notes of the reputed research institutes material, monographs and every source of information etc. He has also to go for conferences for acquiring recent trends in his field, to refer government reports, annual reports, committee reports for acquiring information. One source of information leads to another sources. Hence the researcher should take utmost care in collection of information. A good library will provide every requirement of the researcher. Selection of a good library regarding his area of specialisation is more important for smooth completion of the research project.

(c) Framing the Hypothesis

The researcher should collect all his required information from the various sources and go for in-depth analysis of his research work. The researcher should have a clear vision regarding framing of **"Hypothesis". Hypothesis** is the most important factor in conducting the research problem. **Hypothesis** is a supposition put forward as a basis for reasoning or investigation. The researcher should made assumptions in order to draw out and test its logical or empirical consequences. Research hypothesis are developed and tested as per the synopsis. Hypothesis is a focal point for research and tests must be conducted in the analysis of data. The quality of data occupies a crucial role in testing the hypothesis. In all research projects, the development of working hypothesis plays an important and dominant role. The **hypothesis** must be very specific and limited to the piece of research. It makes the researcher to keep him on the **right track**. It stimulates the thinking levels of the researcher and enhances his abilities to solve the problem more easily and sophisticatedly. The development of working hypothesis is based on the following approach:

(a) A detailed discussion with experts in the field may be useful.
(b) A close interaction with colleagues and other research fellows will be useful.
(c) An in-depth analysis of review of literature may show a right direction in that way.
(d) Verification and examination of data can help in developing the working hypothesis.

In a research project, the interpretation of hypothesis is not necessary. In case of exploratory or formulative research projects do not aim at testing the hypothesis. The working hypothesis must be stated in precise and clearly defined terms. The specification of hypothesis in research project is another basic step of the research process.

(d) Research Design

The identification of the research problem leads the way to go ahead for further work. Research design is the second step in the process of completion of research project. The researcher is required to design his work after identification of research problem. Research design will facilitate the researcher for smooth completion of the research project. It provides for the collection of relevant information with the minimum expenditure and time. Research can be done by the research for the purpose of **"exploration, experimentation, diagnosis and description". Exploration** means a trial to learn about a specific aspect. It is a flexible research design. It provides opportunity for considering many different aspects of problems. It creates accurate description of a situation or a research problem or an association of between variables. The research design should be one that minimise bias and maximises the reliability of the information. **Experimentation** is another kind of research design to test the research problem. **Experiment** is a scientific test to find out or prove something. It is a trial of something new concept. The research problem will be tested on trial base. Experimental design can be further categorised into **informal and formal. Informal** design of research aspect can be applied "before and after without control aspects". **Formal design** of experiment test consists of several methods. These methods are latin square design, block design, randomised design and simple design. The researcher has own choice to select one of the probable method to be selected for execution of his research problem. He must decide himself the method, according to his convenient regarding his research project. **Diagnosis** is an identification of a problem or condition after observing its symptoms. The researcher should prepare his research design. It depends upon several factors such as mode of collection of information availability of research skilled personnel, duration of the project, and the finance available for execution of the research project. Therefore, the researcher should select best method to execute his project.

(e) Selection of Samples

Research means, knowing of truth from a scientific way of method. It is an inquiry for unknown truth from the universe. The process of knowing unknown fact is called research. In the inquiry process regarding obtaining information from the desired sources of information is known as selection of sample. Sample will be collected from universe or population. Inquiry into a problem related area constitute universe or population. **Population** is an inquiry method to collect complete information regarding sample. It is also known as **"Census Inquiry"**. All the relevant factors will be collected by the researcher. In this method all items are covered there is no chance for missing of any information regarding samples. This method shows highest accuracy. However, in practise this may not be true due to some reasons. A slightest element of bias in such inquiry shows a greater impact on observations. However, there is no way of checking the element of bias. This type of inquiry involves a lot of consumption of time, money and other resources. It is useful in some kind of inquiries only. It is not possible for all circumstances. The researcher has to decide the way of selecting a sample. It is popularly known as **"sample design"**. Sample design is the most important factor in determining the collection of data. The collection of data is based on the sampling design adopted by the researcher. The sample will be collected from a given population. **For ex:** The plan to select 14 of a City's 400 retail outlets in a certain way makes a sample design. The way of collection of data is concerned with the requirement of sample design. The samples can be classified as **probability** and **non-probability samples. Probability samples** are based on random sampling. It is a stratified sampling method. It is a systematic and scientific method of sampling. It is a cluster area based method. **Non-probability samples** are based on convenience method of sampling system. They will be included in sample for the convenience of the researcher to complete the research project within stipulated period of time. It is also known as **"Judgement sampling"**. A detailed discussion is necessary for sample design. The following methods of sampling can be classified as:

(i) Simple random sampling method
(ii) Deliberate sampling method
(iii) Area sampling method
(iv) Systematic sampling method
(v) Quota sampling method
(vi) Stratified sampling method
(vii) Complex sample designing method
(viii) Multi-stage sampling method

(i) Simple random sampling method: Simple random sampling method provide for each and every item a chance to inclusion in the sample. Each and every item has equal chance to incorporate in the sample. This method is also known as **Chance sampling**. Each one of the item from universe has the same probability of being selected. It is also called as **"probability sampling"**. **For ex:** If we have to select a sample of **600** items from a universe of **30,000 items**. In this situation, we can select the required sample through **lottery system**. Further all items will be given serial numbers from 1 to 30,000 and 600 five digit random numbers are selected from the table.

(ii) Deliberate sampling method: This method of sampling is called as **Non-probability sampling**. It is also known as **purposive** sampling. It involves the selection of specified units of the universe. If population elements are incorporated in the sample, it is called as **convenience sampling. For ex:** If a researcher wishes to secure data from **fuel buyers,** he may select a fixed number of petrol stations and can conduct interviews at these station. Let us discuss another example. Customer's satisfaction can be found by conducting interviews at the residence of buyers. **Judgement analysis sampling** is another method to select the items from population. It is a qualitative research analysis. It deals with the finding of results regarding qualities of the sample. It requires for development of **Hypothesis**. It do not permit to generalisation. It is always useful to find out the reactions or feelings of the target audience. **For ex:** A judgement sample of **pizza** consumers might be taken to get feelings about **Fast food culture.**

(iii) Area sampling method: Area sampling method is related to selection of samples on the basis of geographical locations. In this method, the total area of interest will be divided into a number of smaller, non-overlapping areas. Hence the researcher will select from these smaller areas are randomly selected. All units in these smaller areas will be included in the sample. It is more useful in making field interviews. The interviewer can do many interviews at each location. It is suitable only when the total geographical area of interest happens to be very big thing. It is quite close to **cluster sampling method**. Cluster sampling method is related to grouping the population. It selects the groups for inclusion in the sample. It do not give priority to the individual elements. **For ex:** A bank wishes to sample its **ATM Card Holders**. It has issued card to **10,000 customers**. The sample is required to be say **300**. For cluster sampling the list of **10,000** could be formed into 100 clusters of 100 card holders each. Three clusters might then be selected for the sample randomly. However, the researcher should ensure higher level of accuracy in procuring sample. This method make the sampling procedure relatively more easier and very smoothly without any interruption of research work. It stimulates the efficiency of fieldwork. It is more suitable for conducting personal interviews.

(iv) Systematic sampling method: The systematic sampling method is related to most practical way of pursuing research projects. It is the best way of selecting sample in some situations. **For ex:**

Select every **10th name** on a list, every **20th** house on one side of the street etc. In this method sample will be selected on randomness. Sample will be picked up by on number basis. It is useful when the sources of data is in the form of a **list**. The picking up of selection of sample starts at random point in the list and then every **Nth** is selected up to required number is secured.

(v) Quota sampling method: Quota sampling is an example of non-probability sampling. It is closely associated with **stratified sampling** method. The researcher has to select the sample from the stratified data. The selection of items will be filled up by the researcher on the allocation of quota method. It is generally happen to take samples on judgement basis. The size of quota is proportionately related to the size of that stratum of the population. The researcher has little freedom in selection of sample.

(vi) Stratified sampling method: Stratified sampling method is useful when the population does not constitute a homogeneous group. Hence the researcher will apply this technique to obtain a representative sample from the population. In this method, the population is divided into a number of **Non-overlapping** sub-population or strata. The sample items are selected from each stratum on random basis. Then it is called as **stratified random sampling method**. It occupies an important and crucial role in selection of representative sample.

(vii) Complex sample designing method: The complex sample designing method is related to mathematical approach. In this method, the sample size is not fixed in advance. It is based as mathematical analysis as the available sources of information. It is useful in statistical quality control aspect.

(viii) Multi-stage sampling method: Multi-stage sampling method is an extension of the cluster sampling. It is associated for conducting research projects on large scale. It is suitable for big enquiries applicable to large geographical areas like entire country. This method covers all geographical locations of a country. In this method the researcher has to select large primary sampling units such as states, districts, towns and ultimately certain families. In this method, the technique of random sampling method will be applied at all stages. However, it is a laborious assignment. It requires to cover entire nation.

Therefore, there are several methods of sampling methods may well be used in the research. Then it is known as **mixed sampling**. Normally a researcher can take random sampling to avoid bias and sampling error can be estimated. Random sampling provide more convenience to the researcher and available at low cost. Hence the selection of sample must be decided by the researcher by taking into considerations of type of inquiry and other related factors.

(f) Collection of Data

Data occupies an important role in pursuing a research project. It is necessary to collect data for a research project in appropriate manner. There are many ways to collect the appropriate data. The process of collecting data in different alternatives leads to save money, time and other resources. The researcher has freedom to collect data in pursuing research project. The sources of information occupies a crucial role in collection of data. The information can be procured in two ways **(a) primary, (b) secondary data**. **Primary data** is the first hand information to the researcher. The researcher collects primary data either through experiments or through **survey**. Experiment system requires observation of quantitative measurements. It helps to examine the fact contained in research hypothesis. **Survey** is the most important device in obtaining the desired data. A survey is a process of collecting data from existing population. It may be either a general purpose survey or a special purpose survey. General purpose survey provide an excellent data for several purposes. **A special purpose survey** is related to study about the specific problem. Proper planning of a survey is most important task before the researcher. The quality of survey results depends upon the preparations made before the conducting of survey. The required data can be procured by the following ways:

(a) Observation method
(b) Schedules method
(c) Personal interview method
(d) Telephone interview method
(e) Questionnaire method

(a) Observation method: Observation method is one of the collections of information by the researcher. In this method information will be procured through observation by the researcher. The researcher will observe happening things without conducting interview with the respondent. This method is quite expensive. It is not a complicated method either past behaviour or future intentions of the research problem. It provides a limited information to the researcher. It is not suitable for inquiries related to large samples.

(b) Schedules method: Schedule method is quite popular in practice. It is one of the method to collect the information through schedules. Schedule is a document sent through enumerators or interviewers. It contains a set of questions which are asked and filled in a face to face situation with another person. The researcher may appoint enumerators to collect information through schedules. It is most useful where informants are illiterate. It provides a high rate of response because of the personal contact of the enumerators. The acquired information is more reliable. This method is involved with high cost. Enumerators will be appointed for this purpose and they are paid persons. The accuracy of data depends largely upon the training imparted to the enumerators. The process of collecting data through schedules requires higher skills and statistical efficiency. The researcher should check the information collected by the enumerators.

(c) Personal interview method: Personal interview method is first hand information related to research problem. In this method, the data will be collected through face to face contact with the informants. The researcher will appoint a number of interviewers as per his requirements. The interviewers will approach the informants and asks them questions relating to the survey and collects the desired information. The information obtained is original in character. This method is useful for intensive field survey. In this method, response is more encouraging. Generally most people are willing to give information when the interviewer approaches them. The information collected through this method is likely to be more accurate, because the interviewer can clear up doubts of the informants about certain questions. It also provides supplement information about informant's personal characteristics. This method is very costly where the number of persons to be interviewer is large. There is a chance of influencing personal prejudice and bias. The interviewers must be highly skilled and trained otherwise the information may mislead the researcher. Untrained or unskilled people may spoil the entire research work. Collecting the information through this method is a time consuming process. Sometimes the investigator may also obtain information on **telephone**. This method is less expensive.

(d) Telephone interview method: In this method, the information will be collected through telephone from the respondents. It is not a very popular method. It plays an important role in industrial surveys for regional development. This method is very useful for time bound research programmes. It is quite less expensive method of investigation. However, this method has some limitations. It is not convenient to collect the information from all respondents because all people may not have own telephone facility. A limited group of people can be approached through this method. In this method, the correspondent has no chance to ask more questions, but very few questions can be asked. It has to be conducted very quickly. The respondents may not give correct answers.

(e) Questionnaire method: Questionnaire method is useful to collect the information from a wide geographical area of locations. It is less expensive method of collection of information. In this method, the information will be collected through a questionnaire. Questionnaire is a document, containing a list of questions related to the survey. It is prepared carefully and sent to the respondents by post. It provide space for every question asked by the researcher to give answer. It will be sent to the informants with a covering letter to fill up the questionnaire and required to sent back it within a specified time. The researcher has to take more cautions while designing the questionnaire. The questionnaire must be prepared without any ambiguity. It can be categorised as structured and non-structured. In case of structured questionnaire, a prescribed sequence of questions is followed. On the other hand, when no prescribed sequence of questions exists, it is called as **non-structured**. The success of this method depends upon many factors. The questionnaire must be very simple. It should not become undue burden on the respondents. It should have prepaid postage facility. It is useful in extensive method of surveys. It should be carefully drafted with utmost care for easy understanding of the asked questions by the informants.

(g) Implementation of Project Work

Implementation of the project is most important stage in the research process. It is also known as execution of the project. The commencement of the research project leads the easy completion without any hurdles. If it proceeds on correct lines in a systematic manner, it will be completed within prescribed time. The duration of the project is another important factor in research process. Generally all research projects are time bound programmes. They should commence and complete within given specified period of time. The researcher should take all precautions to procure better quality of information from the informants. The researcher should provide training to the interviewer. Proper selection and training is the most important step in the research process. The researcher should take necessary steps to smooth collection of information from the informants. If the respondents do not cooperate, some suitable methods to be designed to tackle this problem. The researcher should prepare a list of non-response respondents and with the help of the experts, the problem may be resolved. Therefore, the researcher should take care about accuracy of the data and the survey must be under statistical control.

(h) Analysis of Data

Data is a numerical information. It reflects facts. It provides the progress and decline stage of the things. It is a tool in the hands of a researcher. He uses the data for his research problem. The data will be incorporated in the research project for analysing the problem. The researcher's fundamental task is collection of required data and in turn it should be analysed. The data is raw material for the research project. The analysis of data will be done by the researcher as per his research theme. It requires a number of closely related operations such as classification, tabulation, coding, decoding and their drawing statistical inferences. The researcher should make the data into some purposeful and usable categories. **Editing** is the most important factor in the research project. It improves the quality of data for further coding. Coding stage is ready for tabulation. **Tabulation** is a part of the technical procedure. The simplified and classified data will be put in the form of table. After the introduction of computers in the research areas, all statistical analysis will be done by them. Computers save time and money and helpful to many ways to the researcher. Analysis is the most important factor in execution of the research project. It is based on the computation of various percentages and co-efficients. All statistical tools will be applied for drawing inferences. The researcher should test the hypothesis with the collected information. The validity of data can be verified with the support of all statistical tools.

(i) Testing of Hypothesis

The researcher in pursuing of project, he gathers information, analysis data, drawing inferences from available data and testing hypothesis. Testing hypothesis is occupying a crucial role in study of research problem. The statisticians will apply various tests such as **T Test, F Test, Chi-square Test** for the research purpose. The hypothesis may be tested with anyone or more tests depending upon the nature of the problem. The result will yield either accepting or rejecting it. It is not necessary to reflect our views in hypothesis testing.

(j) Interpretations

Research in social science requires some theoretical approach. Interpretation is the most important stage in the process of research project. After testing of hypothesis, the researcher can arrive to make generalisation to build a theoretical aspect. The researcher's abilities will be reflected in framing of generalisation. Hypothesis testing is not necessary for all research proposals, but it will be helpful to build up theory. If there is no research work contains with hypothesis, the researcher should explain his findings on the basis of same theory. It is called as **interpretation**. Interpretation leads to make further research in future.

(k) Conclusions and Suggestions

After interpretation, the next stage is drafting a thesis. Thesis is a theory put forward and supported by reasoning. It is a lengthy essay submitted for a **University Degree**. The researcher has to prepare the report, with his procured data and relevant information. Drafting of the report is most important factor in the process of research process. The content of a thesis should be like as follows:

(i) Preliminary Pages
(ii) Basic Text
(iii) Closing Matter

(i) Preliminary pages are most important content to get attention towards research work. The researcher should take more care at the introduction stage. The preliminary pages should carry title and date followed by acknowledgements and foreword. The acknowledgements page contains the expression of researcher's feeling towards completion of the project. The researcher must express his compliments to those who have been greatly helpful to him to complete the research project successfully. **Foreword** is another important content in the research thesis or in a report at the initial pages. **Foreword** is an introduction of a book or report or thesis work. The researcher should prepare index of tables and contents and the list of graphs and charts given in the report. The index is more important to a reader to read the content as per his wishes.

(ii) Basic text of the report or thesis should have the following contents:

(a) Introduction
(b) Theme of the report
(c) Findings
(d) Conclusions

(a) *Introduction* is the most important content in the starting pages of the report or thesis or in a book. It provides a simplification process of the subject and easily understandable to even unrelated persons. The researcher's typical task is to present the content to understand by a layman. It is a simplification process and attracts greater attention by the readers. It should contain the objectives of the research, statement of the problems, explanation of methodology and scope of the study. The limitations of the study should also be indicated in this part. The period of research study should be indicated in this part.

(b) *Theme of the report* is another important content in the report or in a book or in a thesis work. The basic content should be presented in a logical sequence. The theme of the report should be divided into various related chapters as per the sequence of the reference. The researcher should make effort to present his research work in chapterisation process. As per the importance of the subject concerned, the researcher can build his work in a related topic wise presentation. The researcher's abilities and experticism may be reflected in the arrangement of presentation of the subject.

(c) *Findings* are another important content of the research project. The researcher should present in a beautiful way to attract the reader. Every person is interested to know the findings of the research.

(d) *Conclusions* are presented in the end of the research theme of the project. The researcher should provide conclusions and suggestions based on his study and experience related to research project. These are the most useful information to the society. All research projects are meant for the purpose of use to society. Society should be benefited with all research works either in social sciences or life sciences. They are more useful to the government, public, corporate sector and others. After completion of the presentation of work, the researcher should put at the end of the report items such as **technical data, bibliography and references.**

(iii) Closing matter contains subject index and vocabulary explanations of the research theme.

Good Research

The ultimate aim of the research is to provide benefits to community. Any research either in social sciences or in life sciences should be able to solve the society problem. The purpose of research is to facilitate better standard of living conditions to the layman. The qualities of a good research is presented below:

(a) Creativity
(b) Logical
(c) Empirical

(a) Creativity is the most important factor in determining the research proposal. The research project should be designed by taking consideration into all factors. It should be structured with well-defined set of rules and build up a sequence in accordance with the goals. The systematic approach of the method does reject the use of guessing and imagination in arriving at conclusions.

(b) Logical presentation of information plays a dominant role in the research process. It implies that research is always based on logical reasoning. **Logic** is a science or a method of reasoning. It makes research more meaningful in the reference of decision making. It consists of two factors i.e., **induction and deduction**. Induction is a process of reasoning applicable from a part to the whole of research project. Deduction is a process of reasoning to be included in conclusion.

(c) Empirical means a work, which is based on observation or experiment. It is not based on theory. Generally research is related to one or more aspects of actual situation. It deals with observed data. Data consists of facts. The facts will be explored in the process of research project. The research result should be verified in accordance with the set of rules.

Problems

Research occupies a dominant role in the developed countries. They concentrate on research and development wings to explore new products and services. A continuous research efforts will bring new items of products and services to make more comfortable to the society. Innovation and creativity occupies a crucial role in determination of a research project. Research activities are not well developed in India due to many factors. Researchers in India are facing several problems which are presented below:

(a) Scientific training
(b) Coordination
(c) Overlapping
(d) Code of conduct
(e) Reference

(a) Scientific Training

Research is occupying a crucial role in the development process of a country. It should be treated as investment avenue to enhance the economic levels of a nation. A strong R&D wings of the corporate sector stimulates the technical capabilities of a nation. Research in social science investigates the new methods to make more comfortable life to the layman. Research in India is completely ignored by the government and private sector. Researchers in India are facing several problems to pursue their research projects. India has a vast population, but lack of proper training to the manpower. There is no availability of trained persons engaged in research work. There is a paucity of competent researchers in India. Researchers in India is in dark without knowing research methods. Most of the research work is not properly followed. In India, the most prestigious research institutes are "Indian Council of Agriculture Research, Regional Research Laboratories, Indian Institute of Chemical Technology, National Institute of Nutrition, Indian Council of Medical Research, Tata Institute of

Fundamental Research, Central Food Research Institute, Indian Institute of Science, National Council of Applied Economic Research, Tata Institute of Social Sciences, Indian Council of Social Science Research, National Institute of Personal Management, Indian Institute of Bankers, National Stock Exchange, ICICI Bank, Export and Import Bank of India, Indian Institute of Finance, Indian Statistical Institute, National Institute of Bank Management.

(b) Coordination

A strong research and development of the corporate sector enables the nation to develop more technologically. Technology occupies a dominant role in the development process of a country. Wealth is only created by technical capabilities. Development is a combination of technology plus financial resources. In India, there is no coordination between industry and universities. In Western countries, there will be good relations between industry and educational institutions. The requirements of the industry needs are fulfilled by the educational institutions. Educational institutions will prepare, guide, supervise and monitored by the experts as per the needs of the industries. There will be a good interaction between industry and educational sectors. Universities are laboratories for the supply of skilled manpower to the corporate sector. Academicians can greatly helpful to the industry at anytime. In India, there should be a strong need to coordinate these two institutions. In pharmaceutical sector, there is an urgent need for a conducting continuous research for exploring new drugs and medicines. India is paying more money towards royalty to the **Multinational Companies** instead of developing its technology. Borrowing technology is more dangerous to the economy rather than for finance.

(c) Overlapping

In India, there is no information is available about current research projects carried out by different organisations. There will be a chance for duplication of research by various organisations. This problem can be solved through a centralised agency for monitoring the activities of research projects. The government should pay proper attention towards identification of research problems regarding various disciplines. Hence repetition and duplication can be avoided.

(d) Code of Conduct

In India, there is no code of conduct for research professionals. Indian Medical Association prepared code of conduct for medical professionals. Institute of Chartered Accountants have prepared its code for practising chartered accountants. Bar Council has its code for practising advocates. But there is no code of conduct for researchers. Hence there is a strong need for developing a code of conduct for researchers.

(e) Reference

Research is based on reference. Libraries provide excellent information to the researcher. Many of our libraries are not in a position to fulfil the needs of researchers. Most of the time and energy of researchers are spent in finding out the books, research journals, research projects and annual publications. Rich libraries are located in New Delhi, Mumbai, Kolkata and Chennai only. The researchers will have to go for their research work to the metros. It is more convenient to the researchers who are located at non-metro cities. Therefore, all information regarding different disciplines should be made available on **Internet**. Online system should be developed and provide this facility on **free of cost** to every researcher. Digital libraries are necessary for the rapid development of all research projects. Some private television channels are also providing excellent information. **For ex: Discovery, NGC, Animal Planet, etc.**

Research Theme

Research means finding facts from unknown. It is an invention process. Nature is a combination of different kinds of resources. The researcher will explore and find many things from the universe. Research is a chasing activity for the unknown. In the process of research, the most important factor is to select properly defined research problem. Identifying research problem is a crucial factor in research process. A researcher must find the problem and solution for the suspected area. Research problem does exist if the following situation arises:

(a) The problem should be related to an individual or a group of persons or an organisation.

(b) There must be at least two courses of action to be studied by the researcher. A course of action is defined by one or more values of the controlled variables.

(c) The research problem should have at least two possible outcomes. One outcome should be preferable to the other. It should have an objective of the study.

(d) The course of action available will provide some chance of getting the objective.

Components

The following factors are determined as components of the research problem:

(i) The problem must be related to an individual or a group of persons or an organisation.

(ii) The research problem must have some objectives to be obtained.

(iii) There must be at least two means of alternatives available to the researcher.

(iv) The researcher should have some doubts in his mind about research problem.

Any research problem carried out by a researcher should provide best solution. There are several other problems which may result in making the problem more complicated.

Identifying the Problem

Research means knowing fact from unknown things. The researcher always thinking about a solution for a complicated problem. His interest is to study the problem in-depthly and provide best solution to the community. Universe is a combination of several unknown elements. Hence the researcher should undertake a research problem after thoroughly identifying the problem. He should undertake the study for providing best solution to the community. In this situation, he may take help from a research guide. The researcher should provide his best solution which cannot be borrowed. A research guide can only help a researcher for selection of a subject. The researcher should take into consideration of the following factors while choosing a research problem or a subject for conducting research.

(a) Identified problem must be innovative and not exposed to the world by any researcher.
(b) The researcher should not touch controversial subject.
(c) The researcher should avoid vague problems.
(d) The researcher should select the best research subject with the help of an expert or a professor in the university department. The expert or a professor may as well read articles published in current journals available as the related subject.
(e) The researcher should also consider other factors such as budget of the project, time factor, data collection, field survey and other problems.

Techniques involved in research problem

Research means exploring new methods from unknown things. Research problem is study of an unexplored solution from the nature. Researcher should prepare the boundary lane within the sphere of research problems. The researcher may study the problem with a pre-determined objective. The problem must be tackled intelligently. The researcher should find a problem and set up techniques for solving the question. Identifying the research problem is most important and crucial factor in research study. All factors should be taken into consideration while defining a research problem. The techniques involved in research problems are presented below:

(a) Statement of the problem
(b) Nature of the problem
(c) Review of literature
(d) Idea generation
(e) Problem analysis

(a) Statement of the Problem

The research study is involved to find a solution to the identified problem. The problem should be stated in a broad general way keeping in view with intellectual interest. The researcher must thorough himself in the concerned subject matter to provide best solutions. In case of social sciences, it is always better to do same field observation.

Field observation is more useful to understand the problem more easily. The researcher may undertake to investigate about the problem in the form of preliminary survey or pilot survey. Therefore, the researcher can get the valuable guidance from the research guide or subject expert. The guide provide his valuable suggestions and guidance in general terms, and it is then up to the researcher to narrow it down and phrase the problem in operational terms. The problem will be narrated by concerned organisational authority that can be indicated accordingly. The indicated problem may contain various ambiguities and it should be resolved by the researcher. The researcher should rethink about the problem with patience and cool thinking over the problem. He has to take all factors into consideration and should try to solve the problem easily. A thorough understanding of the problem enables the researcher to state the problem for easy and quick solution.

(b) Nature of the Problem

The second step in defining the problem is to know about its origin. Before solving the problem, it should be thoroughly understood by the researcher. The researcher should find out the problems root cause originally. He may discuss it with those who have a perfect knowledge regarding the problem. He can make enquiries and collect the suitable information from the sources to resolve the problem. He can take the views of the experts into consideration for in-depth analysis. In-depth analysis of the problem may provide a better way to resolve the origin. The views of the concerned people should also be taken into consideration. Their views cannot be ignored.

(c) Review of Literature

Review of the concerned problems literature occupies an important role in resolving the research query. The researcher should collect the information of concerned problem and it must be surveyed and analysed for a better understanding. Therefore, the researcher must be well conversant with all relevant theories, literature and reports. He should spend sufficient time in review of literature. He may find same information and data regarding the problem. The material which are procured by him is useful for operational purpose. This situation enables the researcher to know the gaps in theories or inconsistent with existing theories. He should also keep in mind about the findings of different studies related to the problem. All these situations will enable the researcher to enhance his knowledge, abilities and skills relevant to the problem. An in-depth analysis of the problem stimulates the abilities of the researcher to provide effective solution.

(d) Idea Generation

Idea is the most important aspect regarding solving a specified problem. It is a plan formed in a human brain. It is a mental impression of the living organism. It leads to establishment of an intellectual property. The researcher should discuss the problem with concerned persons relating to the problem. This situation enables the researcher for easy understanding of the identified problem. Various new ideas can be developed through discussions. **Discussion** is the most important factor in acquiring knowledge regarding a particular aspect. It contains a lot of argument and new things will be explored. Sharing the information with colleagues and concerned people is known as **"experience survey"**. People with rich experience in the related field are in a position to enlighten the researcher regarding the problem. They will be in a position to help the researcher in solving the related problem. They provide best advice and comments to sharpen the efficiency of a researcher. Various ideas regarding a specified problem will be generated in the mind of a committed researcher. He will always think about the problem with the general approach. He should analyse the problem in a different kind of dimensions. His perfection regarding a problem will show an easy way to explore the best solution. He should utilise all the techniques in solving of the problem. Therefore ideas and discussions are more important to the researcher in getting a visible path regarding a research problem. Idea is an outcome of a person's attitude.

(e) Problem Analysis

Analysis means an examination of a specified aspect in detail. The researcher can procure all related information and sit to rephrase the research problem into a working proposition. The researcher, once the nature of problem been thoroughly understood, and the available literature should be surveyed and examined. An in-depth analysis of the problem may help in the framing of **hypothesis**. Hypothesis is an investigation process regarding a particular aspect. The researcher should keep the following points in mind while defining a research problem:

(i) He should use appropriate technical words and terms in the statement of the problem.
(ii) If the study is based on any assumptions, it should be clearly stated in the statement of the problem.
(iii) He should specify the tenure of the research project clearly.
(iv) He should also indicate about the scope of the investigation of the problem. He should demark the limits and horizon of the research work.
(v) He should provide better argument about the selection of statement of the problem. He should explain why the particular study has been taken by him? What circumstance has been made to take up this assignment for pursuing research work.

NOTES

1. Advanced Learners Dictionary, p. 1069, Oxford, 1952.
2. The Encyclopaedia of Social Sciences, Vol. IX. Macmillan, 1930.
3. *Sources*: L.V. Redman and A.V.H. Mory, "The Romance of Research", p. 10, 1923.

UNIT II
DESIGNING OF RESEARCH PROPOSAL

1

RESEARCH DESIGN

Introduction

Research means finding a new thing from unknown. It is a dynamic activity. It is a fact finding enquiry. It is a process of search for knowledge. Knowledge is a commendable force in any kind of environment. It enhances the skills and capabilities of a researcher. It stimulates the abilities of a person. Ability is an inner element to do a thing more perfectly. It is useful in value addition of a specified activity. The solving of a research problem depends upon the research design. The preparation of design of a research project is popularly known as **"Research design"**. Designing of a research proposal contains **"what, where, when, how, why"** elements concerning an inquiry. Research design can be defined as "A research design is the arrangement of conditions for collection and analysis of data in a manner that aims to combine relevance to the research purpose with economy in procedure"[1] . Research design is a conceptual element to commence a project. It is a course of action plan for studying a specified problem. The study shall be completed within the **sphere** of research design. It is a blue print for the collection of data, measurement and observation of the data. Research design includes horizon of research problem and will do writing. The hypothesis from its operational implications of the final analysis. Research design can be classified into **four kinds**: (a) Sampling design, (b) Observation design, (c) Statistical design, (d) Operational design.

Each and every category of design aims to solve the research problems and providing better solution. **Sampling** design is related to the process of collection of sampling items. Sampling items are related to the research theme will be closely observed by the researcher. Researcher will closely associated with the observations of sample items. A detailed discussion is available regarding sampling methods in the forthcoming chapter. **Observation design** is associated with the observation of various items related to research problem. **Statistical design** is related to selection of number of items to be observed for the study. The process of collection of the information and data are also included in the observation the gathered data will be analysed scientifically with the help of various statistical tools. **Operational design** consists of the techniques regarding research problem. It deals with the various procedures specified in the sampling, statistical and research process.

Research design enables the researcher to complete the study more easily. It helps for smooth functioning of the research work. It facilitates the smooth sailing of the various research operations. It completes research process with less amount of expenditure, time and efforts. It is a plan in advance of data collection and analysis of research problem. It is prepared with utmost care because entire research project may upset the study. If the research theme is not properly planned, it does not serve the purpose for which they are undertaken. Sometimes the result of research problem may give misleading conclusions. The entire research exercise may become futile. Hence the researcher should take care about design of the problem. The design contains the ideas of the researcher to solve the problem.

Qualities of a Good Research Design

Research means finding of unknown thing from known facts. For exploring the unknown facts, a good research design is necessary. Research design is a tool in the process of finding unknown facts. It makes the study more sophisticated. It should be more flexible, efficient, economical and appropriate. It minimises the bias and maximise the reliability and accuracy of the collected data. It also makes analysis more scientifically. It should contain less error for best investigation of the research problem. It yields a maximum information and create an environment for providing a better solutions. A good design of research theme can facilitate for easy completion of the study. The question of good design is related to the purpose or objective of the problem. There is no single design of research theme for solving the problem. The design of research theme is different from one study to another. The design may not be useful to all research projects. It is quite different and innovative process. It is an intellectual property. It can be constructed with the help of the researcher's brain. It is involved with creativity. There is no standard formats for carrying out a research project. A good research design involves the consideration of the following elements:

(a) Procurement of required information and data.
(b) Qualities, capabilities and skills of the researcher and his staff.
(c) The basic objectives of the study.
(d) Funding process and tenure of the research project.

A good research design is always helpful to the researcher and it must be in flexible as per the needs of the study. The research study contains many new elements, ideas, insights and based on foresight of the future generations. The research study should concentrate not only current problems but also it must emphasis as future generation. The study must be useful for not only for present but also for future. Accuracy in carrying out research study occupies a dominant role in designing a good research theme. A good research design reduce the bias and stimulate the reliability of the study. A research study involving the testing of hypothesis between variables may lead to minimise the bias. A scientific analysis is always maximise the reliability of the study. However, we can say that a good research design is a tool for easy completion of the research work and a guiding force for the future research workers. Research is a continuous process.

Basic concepts in research design

Research design is the important task before a researcher. A good design will reduce the hurdles and problems of the study. We cannot ignore the importance of a research study. Research design can be described as a drawing of a plan for construction of a building. The comfort and beauty of the building depends upon the sketching of a good plan. Drawing of a good plan is based on efficiency and skills of the architecture. A good research design will be outcome of a good research worker. The research should have some ideas and concepts while drawing a design for a study. The following concepts may be useful to the researcher in preparation of design:

(a) Variables
(b) Hypothesis
(c) Experiments

(a) Variables

Variable means a part of element liable to change. It refers to changeable attitude. It is not a constant aspect. It is involved with quantitative values. The concepts like income, height, weight are all examples of variables. It is more useful in quantitative analysis. It contains the numerical expression of a particular aspect. Quantitative analysis deals with the description of numerical data. Qualitative analysis is also stratified into the numerical expression. Variables can be classified as **"dependent and independent"**. Dependent variable means a variable which depends upon other variables. **For ex:** The relation between height and age can be observed as dependent and independent variable. Height depends upon age. Height is called as dependent variable. **Independent variable** means a variable that is antecedent to the dependent variable. It is not related to the purpose of the study. It may influence the dependent variable. Variables further can be classified as **continuous and non-continuous variable**. Continuous variable means, a phenomena which can take as quantitative analysis basis. It can assume as any expression of numerical value within a specified range. **For ex:** Age is a continuous variable. **Non-continuous variables** are also known as discrete variables. It can be expressed in integer values. **For ex:** number of children. "A variable for which the individual values fall on the scale only with distinct gaps is called a discrete variable. **Independent variable** is also known as **extraneous variable**. It is not related to the purpose of the research study. It may show impact on dependent variable. A good research is always minimise the influence of independent variable. Independent variables are always works under control. Control is used to refer to restrain experimental conditions.

(b) Hypothesis

Hypothesis is a predictive statement. It is involved for investigation of a fact. The fact should be tested by scientific methods. It is termed as **Research hypothesis**. It is related to an independent variable to a dependent variable. Researcher hypothesis is a combination of one independent and are dependent variable. Every research hypothesis must be tested scientifically. If it is not tested scientifically, it is not termed as research hypothesis. The basic aim of the research is to test scientifically of a fact. If a research theme contains hypothesis for testing, it is termed as **"hypothesis testing research"**. It can be of the experimental design or of the non-experimental design. A research theme which contains independent variable is known as **"experimental hypothesis testing research"**. If a research theme does not contain independent variable is called as **Non-experimental "hypothesis testing research"**. **For ex:** A researcher wants to know the IQ and reading abilities for a group of children. For this purpose he randomly selects 100 childrens and test their intelligence and reading ability through calculation of correlation between two elements. It is an example of non-experimental testing research.

(c) Experiments

Experiment means a scientific test to find out or prove something. It is the process of examining the truth of a statistical hypothesis. **For ex:** We can conduct an experiment to examine the usefulness of a training programme for workers. Experiments can be categorised into two methods **(a) absolute experiment, (b) comparative experiment**. Absolute experiments are useful to determine the impact of a specified aspect. **For ex:** If the researcher wants to determine the impact of a drug for patients is known as absolute experiment. If we want to determine the impact of one drug to another drug for comparison is called as comparative experiments. A group is exposed while conducting experimental hypothesis testing to usual conditions. It is known as **"control group"**. It is also termed as experimental group. Treatment is one of the important factor in experimental hypothesis testing. The experimental and group elements are put usually in treatment situation. A close observation of all affairs under the experiment method can be termed as **"treatment"**. **For ex:** Study of impact of fertilisers in cultivation of land. A treatment of different combinations are termed as **"experimental units"**. They are pre-determined blocks. These units must be selected very carefully.

Kinds of Research Design

Research means tracing out of the unknown factor from the known. A good research design may facilitate for easy completion of the study. The efficiency and abilities are reflected in the designing of a good research theme. It should be prepared more carefully to study the research problem. Research designs will be prepared as per the study of a problem. However, different research designs can be classified as per the convenient of the researcher as follows:

(a) Exploratory research studies
(b) Descriptive research studies
(c) Hypothesis testing research studies

(a) Exploratory Research Studies

A good research design is always helpful to the researcher. Exploratory research study is also called as formulative research studies. It is a more precise investigation process. It is involved in developing the working hypothesis. It focuses on formulating a problem. It emphasizes on the discovery of ideas and foresight. The research study must be designed as flexible as to provide better solutions to the research problem. Research design must be based on study of the problem, collection of data and broad aspects. Usually the following three methods can be taken into consideration while preparing exploratory research studies:

(a) Review of literature
(b) Experience survey
(c) Intensive study

Review of literature is an important factor in designing of exploratory research studies. A close study of survey of relevant literature enables the researcher to understand the research problems very quickly. It is the most simple and fruitful method. It helps in formulating the research problem or developing hypothesis. The researcher can learn from the earlier hypothesis works and enables him for further movements. He can review the past research work and provide a way for further research work. The bibliography is more useful for the researcher for precisely formulating the problem.

Bibliography is a list of books about a subject or by a specified author. It provides full information with all relevant concepts and theories, research articles published recently in various journals regarding a specified subject. The published work of creative writers provide a good base for hypothesis formulation.

Experience survey is associated with practical experience people related to the research problem. The aim of survey is to know the relationships between variables to be studied research problem. The researcher should select a best survey people with competent skills and generate new ideas. The respondents who are selected by the researcher will be interviewed by the survey people. The researcher should design a good interview schedule for the systematic collection of information. However, the respondents should be allowed sufficient freedom to raise issues and questions related to the research problem. The investigation should have best experience in collection of information through interview method. The researcher should provide a copy of the questions to be discussed to the respondents in advance. Therefore, the respondent can acquire same knowledge and easily he can face the interview. **Insight analysis** is useful for formulation of hypothesis for research. It is also known as **intensive study**. Intensive study consists of selected instances of the aspect related to research problem of interested. The collection of information may be done through unstructured interview or some other method may be adopted. The study depends upon many factors such as attitude of the investor abilities of the researcher and intensity of the study. The selection of problems or examples of the research project may depend upon the circumstances around the researcher.

Therefore, exploratory research studies may lead to development of hypothesis. Research design is an important factor for completion of the project without any hurdle. Research design must remain to be flexible when different kinds of problems arise and come to the notice of the researcher. Researcher skills, investigator's abilities and staff members' attitude will occupy an important role in completion of a research project. However, the researcher should be ready to face any difficulties or to face any hurdle in completion of his research project.

(b) Descriptive Research Studies

Descriptive research studies are associated with the close observation of characteristics of a particular individual or a group of persons. It is related to study about the individual characteristics consisting of specific predictions and narration of facts. All research projects comes under this category. The researcher should be able to define clearly regarding his scientific investigation for measuring it along with a clear idea of population. The research design must make all sufficient provisions to make complete information about the study. The research design must be rigid and consist the following elements:

(i) Framing of the objective of the study
(ii) Provision of best method for collection of data
(iii) Selection of sample
(iv) Processing and examination of the data
(v) Findings and conclusions

(i) Framing Objectives: Research means searching for unknown fact from the universe. There are several methods to conduct research projects i.e., observation, questionnaire, interviewing and verification of records, etc. These methods have their merits and limitations. The researcher has freedom to select one or more of these methods for completion of the study. The researcher should take all precautions before design research theme. He should give top priority for framing the objectives of the study. In descriptive research studies, the first step is to specify the objectives with sufficient information. The data must be collected from relevant source with scientific approach. If it is not done in a systematic way, the study may not yield desired information. Hence the researcher should frame his research objectives as per the available resources. The identification of research problem must be innovative and creating interest to the layman. Any research project in any discipline should show impact on the life style of a layman.

(ii) Collection of data: The aim of the research study depends upon the quality of relevant data. Data contains the numerical expression regarding a particular aspect. It is reflected in characterisation of a phenomenon. It is also useful in qualitative aspects of the research study. The researcher should take care about the collection of data regarding his proposed research project. He should take care while designing the research theme. He should design the method of data collection with adequate safeguard against bias and unreliability must be ensured. The questions must be designed without any ambiguity and investigators should be instructed not to express their own opinion in conducting of interview. The investigators must be provided sufficient proper training in collection of data. The researcher should apply all precaution tests to pre-test the data collection for post results.

(iii) Selection of sample: All research projects are based on the study of relevant samples of the problem. The samples are useful to the researcher for making statement of the problem of population. Samples may yield accurate information with a minimum effort of research skills. In collection of data, the field staff should be more careful and perform their duty honestly. They are responsible for collection of error free data from the population. It is necessary to supervise the research staff for accuracy in collection of samples. Usually the researcher may select one or more forms of sampling methods.

(iv) Processing and examination of data: After the collection of sample, the next step is to process the collected information into a finished product form. The collected data is a raw material for the researcher. The material will be purified according to the needs and convenient for the research study. The collected data must be processed and analysed scientifically. The processing of data includes various steps such as coding the interview replies observations, tabulation of data and applying various statistical tools. The researcher should be more careful in this stage of research work. It is the most important stage, because data will be processed through different methods to arrive better results. Any ignorance in this stage may cause the wrong result from the research work. Hence the researcher should prepare a detailed plan before commencing the research work. This situation may prove in economical sense and it may avoid unnecessary labour.

(v) Findings and conclusions: The researcher has to apply various statistical tools for arriving accurate results. Research is a process to find out new things from the universe. The unexplored facts may be exposed to the public. Universe is a combination of different exposed and unexposed elements. All the hidden facts are exposed to the public through various research projects. Researchers are pulling out the hidden facts from the nature. The important task of the researcher is to communicate the findings to the society. The arrived result must be useful to the society. The fruits of research results should change the life styles of the layman. The researcher should present his findings in a systematic manner for better understanding of the problem. The presentation of information in a good manner is the efficiency for the researcher's skills and abilities. He has better communication abilities in expression of his findings. He should explain how far his research findings are useful to the society. The researcher has the social responsibility in providing solution to the problems faced by the society. He is the guiding force for solving the prolonged problems faced by the society. He should provide some relief to the society by exploring new facts and solutions. Researchers in life science and social sciences can definitely change the lives of crores of people by taking research as a·challenging task.

(c) Hypothesis testing research

Hypothesis means a supposition put forward as a basis for investigation of a problem. It may not be necessarily true factor. It is known as **experimental study**. The researcher test the hypothesis of casual relationships between variables. Hypothesis studies reduce bias and increase reliability and useful in drawing inferences. A research project which contains hypothesis testing may yield better inferences from the experiments. Experimental designs are conducted by **Prof. R.A. Fisher**. These studies are originated from Agriculture Research in England. **Prof. Fisher** is also associated with the experimental design. He had conducted several experiments related to agriculture field. This situation enables him to develop certain experimental designs for testing hypothesis related to scientific investigation. At present all research projects related to all disciplines are being used hypothesis testing. The facts are tested with scientific approach for better reliability of the result. Experimental designs are not only useful to life sciences but also to humanities disciplines. **Prof. R.A. Fisher** has closely related to these designs. He has categorised experimental designs based on three principles. They are presented below for further discussions:

(i) Replication
(ii) Randomisation
(iii) Local Control

(i) Replication means conducting an experiment in several times. The experiment should be repeated more than once. By repeating the same experiment, the statistical accuracy may be increased. **For ex:** Suppose we can examine the effect of two varieties of wheat. The field can be divided into two parts, allocating each field for each variety of wheat. We can compare the yield of the two parts and draw the inferences from the conducted experiment. If we are to apply the principle of **replication** to this experiment, we have to first divide the agricultural field into several parts, grow one variety in one part and another variety in the remaining part. We can compare two fields yield from the collected data. We can draw the conclusions regarding yield of these two parts. The result obtained from these experiments will be more reliable in comparison. The entire experiments can be repeated several times for better results. The **principle of replication** increases the accuracy and validity of the results. It does not create any problem, but it creates while computations involved in the experiment.

(ii) Randomisation is one of the basic principles of experimental designs. It provides protection from the external factors. It is a cushion against the effects of extraneous factors. It provides safety by combining all extraneous factors under the general classification of chance. Chance factor occupies an important factor in conducting an experiment. **For ex:** If we grow one variety of wheat in the first half of the part of a land and another variety is grown on the another part of land, then the yield of produce depends upon the fertility of the soil. In this situation we may assign the variety of wheat may be grown in different parts of the field on the basis of random sampling technique. Hence the application of randomisation principle can reduce the experimental error. It indicates a reliable result of comparison between two variables.

(iii) Local control is another important principle of experimental designs. It is associated with elimination of error from the experimental method. The variability in results of the experiment can be measured and eliminated. As per the principle of local control, we first divide the agriculture field into various parts. Each part again divided into equal sub-parts for growing of wheat. Thus the experiment should be started randomly on these different parts of blocks. The blocks are measured with the yield output by experiment process. Hence we can measure its contribution to the total variability of the data through analysis of variance.

Kinds of experimental designs

Research means, searching for a solution to the existing problem. It provides answer to the problem faced by the community. Every research project shall provide a solution to the society's burning problems. Researchers should also feel the responsibility to the problems faced by the community. They are intellectuals, highly qualified and skill persons, should spend their manpower towards solving the society's problems. The government, large public organisations, non-government organisation should also participate in various research programmes. All these organisations should encourage scientists towards providing solutions to the society. Therefore, the necessary of experiments cannot be ignored. Experimental design is related to the conceptual framework of an experiment to be conducted for a specific purpose. Experimental design can be classified into two kinds, which are presented below for further discussions.

(A) Informal experimental design
(B) Formal experimental design

(A) Informal experimental design

Informal experimental designs are associated with less sophisticated form of analysis. The analysis will be based on various factors such as differences in magnitudes. Informal experimental designs can be categorised as follows:

(a) Before and after without control design
(b) After only with control design
(c) Before and after with control design

(a) Before and after without control design: In this method variables are measured before the introduction of treatment. Experiment will be designed to study the impact of the variables. For conducting experiments a single test group or area is selected. The treatment will be commenced and analysis will be made before treatment and after treatment. The impact will be closely observed and recorded. The effect of the treatment will be computed as the level of the phenomenon after the treatment **minus** the level of the phenomenon before the treatment. The impact will be computed through the following formula:

$$\text{Impact} = \begin{matrix}\text{Level of phenomenon} \\ \text{before treatment} \\ \text{(X)}\end{matrix} - \begin{matrix}\text{Level of phenomenon} \\ \text{after treatment} \\ \text{(Y)}\end{matrix}$$

$$\text{Impact} = Y - X$$

(b) After only with control design: In this method, two groups or variables will be selected for conducting experiment. The two groups can be categorised as **test area and control area**. The experiment or treatment will be introduced in test area only. After the treatment is commenced, the dependent variable would be measured in both the areas of the same time.

Test area =	Commencement of treatment	–	Level of phenomenon after treatment (A)
Control area	→		Level of phenomenon without treatment (B)

Impact of Treatment = A – B

(c) Before and after with control design: In this method, the experiment design will be prepared in accordance with the requirement of study of impact of the treatment. For conducting experiment, two areas are selected for observation. The dependent variable is measured in both the area before commencing treatment. The treatment is introduced into the test area only. The dependent variable can be measured before and after the introduction of the treatment. The treatment impact can be computed as follows:

Treatment impact = (A – B) – (C – D)

Test area:	Time period I Level of phenomenon before treatment (B)	Time period II Level of phenomenon after treatment (A)
Control area:	Level of phenomenon without treatment (D)	Level of phenomenon without treatment (C)

(B) Formal experimental design

Formal experiment designs are conducted relative with more control. It uses more precise statistical tools and procedures for making good analysis of the experiment. The aim of the experiment is to study the impact of treatment as the dependent variable. The formal experimental designs can be categorised as follows:

(i) Completely randomised design
(ii) Randomised block design
(iii) Latin square design
(iv) Factorial design

(i) Completely Randomised Design

This method is popularly known as **(CR Design)**. It involves principle of replication and randomisation of experimental designs. It is easiest and simplest method for analysis. It is based on randomly assigned to experimental treatments. **For ex:** If we have 20 elements and if we want to test 10 elements under treatment X and 10 under treatment Y, the randomisation process provides a group of 10 elements selected from a set of 20 an equal opportunity under treatment X and Y. The treatment of impact can be studied through **one way analysis of variance**. In this method all the extraneous factors will be included in the chance of variation. This experiment design can be further classified as follows:

(a) Two group design method
(b) Random replication design

(a) Two group design method: This method is useful for studying behavioural sciences. It is the simplest method. It is useful for comparison of two groups of variables. It does not control the extraneous variables. The result of this experiment may not depict a correct picture. In this method, first step involves to define the population. From the population, a sample is selected randomly. The selected item will be assigned to the experimental and control groups. This method yields a two groups as representatives of the population. This situation enables to draw conclusions and inferences as the basis of samples collected from the defined population. **For ex:** If we want to compare two groups of children's who have been randomly selected and assigned. The impact of coaching can be analysed through this method. The impact of children before giving coaching and after giving coaching.

(b) Random replication design: In this method the extraneous variable was not controlled. Replication of experiment is called as **"Replication"**. In this method samples are selected as random basis. The dependent variable were ignored in this design. Random replication design is an extension of the two group sample randomised design. The design provides differential effects of the extraneous independent variables. It elevates any individual differences among the variables conducting an experiment. In this design, there are two populations, one sample is taken randomly from the population available for study. Another sample is taken randomly from the population available to conduct experiments for selected group. Usually equal number of items will be put in each group and the size of the group may not effect the result of the study.

(ii) Randomised block design

Randomised block design contains the principle of local control. It can be applied with other two principles of experimental designs. In this method subjects are divided into blocks. The block is a combination of homogeneous characteristic variables. The sample selected for grouping the subject is related to the measure to be obtained in respect of the dependent variable. The experiment will be conducted in all blocks. One subject in each block would be randomly assigned to each treatment. This design is analysed by analysis of variables.

(iii) Latin square design

Latin square design is one of the experimental methods in pursuing research studies. It is very frequently used in agricultural research. Agricultural research investigations are different from other studies. In agriculture nature plays an important role in cultivation. The experiments will be conducted in study of fertility in soil in different parts of the selected sample area. The output of the cultivation is effected by number of factors such as **fertilisers, seeds, soil and climate**. Latin square design is similar to the two-way analysis of variance technique. It is useful for comparison of different kinds of seeds, soils and fertilisers.

(iv) Factorial design

Factorial design is useful in pursuing research problems related to several economic and social aspects of the nation. In this method the experiments will be conducted for observing the effect of more than one factor. Factorial design can be categorised into two methods:

(a) Simple factorial design
(b) Complex factorial design

(a) Simple factorial design: Simple factorial design is associated with the study of effect of two factors as the dependent variable in experiment method. It is also known as two factor factorial design. It can also be called as **2 × 2** simple factorial design. In this method, there will be two variables i.e., experimental variable and control variable. The treatment will be at two levels. In this design we can study the main effects of treatment and the main effects of levels.

(b) Complex factorial design: Complex factorial design is involved in study of effect of more than two factors on the dependent variable in experiment method. It considers three or more independent variables at the same time conducting experiment. It is also known as **2 × 2 × 2** complex factorial design. In this design it is possible to determine the main effects for three variables. This design provides accuracy with less labour and is also a source of economy for the project.

NOTE

1. Claire Sellitz, Research Methods in Social Sciences, p. 50, 1962.

2

SAMPLING DESIGN

"Wisdom is knowing what to do next, Skill is knowing, how to do it, And virtue is doing it."

Introduction

Research means knowing or learning from nature. It is a process where lakhs of inquiries made for unknown things. The nature is termed as **Universe**. Universe is termed as **population**. Population contains all items in the field. Universe is a reflection of several elements which are hidden in the nature. The hidden facts in the universe are explored by the researchers. The researchers are always working for exploring new avenues, new techniques, new ways and new methods for providing sophisticated life to the layman. Before nature, the man is always innocent and he is searching for unknown things. Nature has all solutions for all problems. The research process provides the way for finding solutions to the problems. Hence the universe contains problem and simultaneously solution. The task of researcher is exploring facts from the universe. A complete evolution of all items in the universe is known as **census inquiry**. Census inquiry covers all items. No item will be left and most accuracy is obtained. It is the most important method for conducting an in-depth analysis. But in practice it is not possible to cover all items. A small error caused in experiment may lead to damage the result. Hence samples should be checked and all precautions be taken for error free result. Sample means, a small part showing the quality of the whole. But there is no way or methods to check the samples. It will be checked through resurvey or use of sample checks. Census inquiry involves a great deal of time, money and energy. It is not possible to do research in this method. It is possible to the government only. Even government sometimes cannot adopt this method due to certain problems. In same situations this method may not be helpful to the researcher. **Sample survey** is another kind of field survey. Field studies are more useful in routine life. In this method, time, cost and selection of respondents elements will occupy a greater role in designing of the research. Among other things the selection of respondent is a crucial factor for commencing the study. The respondents should be selected from the representative of the total population. The selected respondents may be called as **sample** and the selection process is known as **sampling technique**. The method of conducting the survey is known as **sample survey**. The researcher has to decide the sample size and design for completion of the project.

Sample Design

The process of selection and collection of data from population is known as **sample**. Sample design is a plan for collection of a sample from universe. It lays down the number of items to be selected from the universe. It is decided in advance before going to data collection. The researcher has freedom to choose the sample design. He has to select best sample design method and appropriate for his research study. Sample design involves many steps which are presented below:

(a) Objectives
(b) Unit
(c) Sources
(d) Sample size
(e) Funding sources
(f) Area of interest
(g) Process of sampling

(a) Objectives

The researcher has to move according to his research theme. The first step in framing of sample design depends upon the objectives of the study. The study should be made from the universe. The universe is a reflection of many combination of elements. The sample design indicates the number of items to be studied in research project. Universe can be categorised as **finite** or **infinite**. In **finite**, the universe has certain number of items. But in case of **infinite**, there is no certain number of items. We cannot say or estimate about the total number of items in the universe. **For ex:** The population of Mumbai city, the number of students in a university are the best examples for **Finite Universe**. The best examples for **Infinite Universe** is the number of animals in the nature, stars in the sky, throwing of a dice etc.

(b) Unit

Research means exploring new aspects or things from the nature. The researcher has to select the sample from universe or population. A sampling unit must be decided before selecting sample. Sampling unit is related to a geographical area or an economic unit or a social unit. The researcher can select his sample as per the requirement of his study.

(c) Sources

After selection of sample, the researcher has to procure the information for his research study. All the required material is available from the universe and researcher has to find out unknown things from the known facts. Universe is based on logic. All items are hidden in the universe, the human being is trying to exploring the unknown elements. The knowing of unknown resources is termed as sampling frame. The researcher has to prepare the sources himself. A list which is prepared by the researcher must be comprehensive, correct, reliable and accuracy.

(d) Sample size

Research is a process to find out new things from the universe. Universe contains all the items which are known and unknown by the man. The unknown elements are explored by the researcher. The unknown facts are known through selection of some sample. Sample is the representative of the whole. The sample can be selected randomly. The researcher has to decide the size of sample to be taken from universe for his study. The number of items constitute a sample. The researcher has freedom to determine the number of items to be included in his study. He should take care about the size of sample. The size of sample should not be more in large and not in small. The size of sample should be ideal. The sample level must be optimum and it should be in required characters. The optimum sample must be reliable, flexible, efficiency and representative of the whole. The researcher should also keep in mind about the funding amount while determining the size of sample. The determination of size of sample is influenced by many factors. Hence the researcher has think about all his circumstances regarding his experiment. Budget is one of the important factor in framing of research study.

(e) Funding sources

Fund plays an important role in research study. The study will be completed smoothly, if sufficient funds are deployed. If any interruption in flow of funds to the research study, the experiment will be disturbed. The research work will be vain. Budgetary constraint is one of the important element in smooth functioning of research study. The researcher has to coordinate all the things with the funding agency or nodal agency for implementation.

(f) Area of interest

Sample is a representative of the element for the whole. The determination and process of collection is termed as **sampling design**. The selection of sample from the universe depends upon the area of research interest. **For ex:** we may be interested in finding the costliest city in the world from the various samples of parameters.

(g) Process of sampling

Researcher has full freedom in pursuing of his research study. He has to determine the selection of sample for his research. He has to decide the size of sample to be collected from different sources of information. He has to apply all techniques to collect the required data. There are several techniques available for collection of data. Hence the researcher has to go further step for sampling procedure for commencement of his research project work.

Sampling procedure

Sample occupies a dominant role in making a research project with great success. Sample selection is an important factor for easy understanding of the research problem. The researcher must decide the sampling procedure for continuously conducting an experiment without any interruption. Sample is the raw material for the researcher. The researcher will make finished product with his available raw material. The researcher has to keep in his mind about two factors regarding sampling procedure. They are involved in cost factor. The researcher must think about the cost involved in collection of data and incorrect inferences from the acquired data. The acquired data will be synthesised as per the research theme and the result will be absorbed in the study. The result should be accurate and must consist of relevant information. The incorrect inferences may be arises due to same factors. They are called as **systematic bias and sampling error**. A systematic bias cannot be reduced. It cannot be avoided by increasing any sample size. The incorrect inferences may be caused in a research problem by the following factors:

(A) Systematic bias
(B) Sampling error

(A) Systematic bias

Sample is the raw material for researcher. He has to select carefully his raw material for producing finished·product with more quality. Any inferior quality in raw material may lead to the inferior output. The quality of the output depends upon the introduced input. Sometimes errors cannot be eliminated by the researcher. In same situations errors may be detected and corrected by the researcher. Systematic bias results in the following situations:

(i) It results, if a biased representation of the universe.
(ii) It results, when a questionnaire or the interviewer is biased.
(iii) It results, when the selected samples do not express interest.
(iv) It results, when the observation kept as individuals, their attitude will be changed.
(v) It results, when the data relates income tax and financial aspects of the individuals.

(B) Sampling error

Sampling errors occur randomly. It can be decreased by adjusting the size of sample. It can be measured for a given sample design and size. The sample error can be measured through **"precision of the sampling plan"**. A large quantum of sample enhances the systematic bias. Hence the researcher has to increase the precision of sampling through better sampling design.

Kinds of Sample Design

Sample is the representative characteristics of the universe. The designing for collection of sample is termed as **"sample design"**. There are different kinds of sample designs exist in practice, i.e.,

(a) Probability sampling
(b) Non-probability sampling

Probability sampling is related to random selection. The process of selection of sample through random basis method is termed as **probability sampling**. It is also known as **random sampling**. Further it may be termed as **"chance sampling"**. In this method, every item of the universe has a chance to include in the sample. This method ensures the law of statistical regularity. The individual units are picked up from the universe for conducting an experiment. The sample units will be picked up from lottery method. There is no chance to select specified unit of sample for making an experiment. The obtained result from the experiment shows the most accuracy with valid impact. The random sampling is the best technique for selecting a representative sample. We can measure the errors of estimation. It avoids personal bias of the investigator. It can be further divided into two methods.

(a) Lottery method
(b) Table number

Lottery method is a very popular method in statistical inquiry. Under this method, all items of the universe are numbered or named as separate slips of paper in similar size and shape. All the slips are mixed with a speed and put in a container or drum. A blindfold selection is made among all the samples. **For ex:** If we want to select 20 samples from 200 persons, 200 slips should be prepared and mixed in drum. From the containers, a blindfold selection of 20 slips will be picked up for selection. This method is very popular in distribution of and selection of prizes. The researcher should take all precautions in variation of size and shape of papers.

Table number is an alternative method of lottery method. The random table numbers are obtained by a specified process. According to the method, the sample will be selected from tables. The tables contains a random sequence of the digits **0 to 9**. There are several standards of random numbers are available, among them **five** methods are extensively tested for randomness. They are presented below:

(1) Tippets random numbers
(2) Fisher and Yates random numbers
(3) Kendall and Babington Smith
(4) Rand Corporation
(5) CR Rao random numbers

Tippets random numbers are mostly popular in practice. This table was introduced in 1927 and consisting of **41600** random digits grouped into **10400** sets. These digits have set of four-digit random numbers. These set of four digits have been subjected to numerous tests and used in many investigations. Their accuracy has been well established for all practical purposes. The following set of four digits are best example for Tippets random numbers:

2952	2754	9143	1112	2762	7203	5911	6111	4233
4167	9524	3992	1405	6107	3563	5356	3170	8816
2670	7483	1545	9792	9025	6008	1089	1300	5624
0560	5246	3408	1396	7969	7002	8125	6913	2693
						7691	8776	6446

From the above table, we have to select 20 items from 6000. Then we have to adopt a procedure to number all the 6000 items from **1 to 6000.** Tippet table may then be consulted and the first twenty numbers up to 6000 may be noted down. From the table the following portion of the digits will be adopted:

2952	3992	5911	3170	5624	4167
1545	1396	5356	1300	2693	2370
3408	2762	3563	1089	0560	5246
1112	4233				

The above set of digits constitute the sample. According to the sample table, the universe can be classified into two methods: **(a) uni-**

verse size less than 1000 and (b) less than 100. If the universe size less than 1000 and our desired sample is 10 items out of 400. All items from 1 to 400 should be numbered as **001 to 0400**, we may now select 10 numbers from the table up to 0400.

If the universe size is less than 100, the table may be used as follows:

29	52	66	41	39	92	97	92	79	69	
59	11	31	70	56	24	70	56	24	41	67

Ignoring the numbers greater than 80, we obtain ten random numbers, namely 29, 52, 66, 41, 39, 92, 97, 92, 79, 69, 59, 11, 31.

Fisher and Yates table was introduced in 1938. The table contains random number of **15000**. The digits are arranged into 1500 sets of ten digit random numbers. These table consists of 300 blocks, each block consisting of 4 rows and 5 columns.

Kendall and Babington Smith table was introduced in 1939. The table consists of 1,00,000 random digits grouped into 25,000 sets of four digit random numbers. This method of random selection cannot be useful in case of articles wheat, petrol, ghee, etc.

Rand Corporation table was introduced in 1955. The table contains 1,00,000 random digits categorised into 20,000 sets of five digit random numbers.

C.R. Rao table was introduced in 1966. It contains random numbers.

Probable sampling method consists of two kinds: **(a) unrestricted sampling method, (b) restricted sampling method**. Unrestricted sampling method is also termed as **Random sampling**. Further restricted random sampling method can be divided into following methods:

(a) Stratified sampling
(b) Systematic sampling
(c) Cluster sampling

(a) Stratified Sampling

Stratified random sampling is also known as simple stratified sampling method. It is related to obtain a representative sample. Representative sample contains the relevant characteristics of the population in the same proportion and the sample includes population. If a population from which a sample is to be drawn does not constitute a homogenous group. Then the stratified sampling can be applied for obtaining representative sample. Under this method, the population will be divided into several sub-populations. The sub-population of different kinds is called as **"strata"**. Then the researcher will select each item from each strata to constitute a sample. This method is more reliable and with high accuracy. It is estimated with more accurate each component of the sample. The characteristic of the components of the sample is the most important factor. The data should be divided on the basis of similar characteristics. Strata should be constructed to reduce the differences among sampling units within strata. The researcher should also think about the number of stratas to be classified. As a general perception less than 06 stratas is desirable. The researcher must think about regarding consideration of number of observation in his experiment. For deciding the quantum of observations, the researcher can use either a **proportional or a disproportional** allocation method. In proportional method of allocation, one sample will be taken from each strata in proportion to its relative weight. **Indisproportional method**, the different strata are sampled at different rates. The variation of the measurements differs greatly from strata to strata.

(b) Systematic Sampling

Systematic sampling is known as **quasi-random** sampling method. It is easier and less costlier method of sampling. It can be conveniently used even in case of large populations. It is spread more over the entire population. This method is to select every **"ith"** item as a list. An aspect of randomness is introduced into this method by using random numbers to pick up the unit which to commence. **For ex:** If a 5 per cent sample is desired, the first item would be selected randomly from the first twenty and thereafter every 20th item would automatically be included in the sample. Hence the 1st item of the sample and the remaining units of the samples are selected at a fixed interval. This method of sampling is not preferable in all situations.

(c) Cluster Sampling

Cluster sampling is related to simple random sampling. The random selection is made of primary, intermediate and ultimate units from a given population. There are several stages in the cluster sampling method. At the first stage, the units are acquired through same suitable method. In the second stage, the units are selected from the first stage sample units, through some suitable methods. Further stages may be processed as per the requirement of the study. **For ex:** If we want to take a sample of 10,000 households from Andhra Pradesh. At the first stage, the A.P. state may be divided into a number of districts and some districts selected at random. At the second stage, each district may be divided into a number of villages and a sample of villages may be taken at random. At the third stage, a number of households will be selected from each of the villages selected from the second stage process. This method introduces flexibility in sampling process. It permits the fieldwork to be concentrated and yet large area to be covered. It is more useful particularly valuable in surveys of underdeveloped areas. However, it lacks from accuracy of the sample. This method is best suitable for conducting research studies, where big area of geographical locations to be studied. This method reduces cost by concentrating surveys in selected clusters. It is used due to economic advantage which it possesses.

However, many methods are available to the researcher to select sample for his research study as per the convenience. It should be noted that no one method can be regarded as best under all circumstances each method has its own advantages.

Size of Sample

Size of sample is an important factor in research study. Adopting a sampling technique depends upon the size of sample. Size of sample means the number of sampling units selected from the population for investigation. The size of sample have been defined by different experts in different ways. **For ex:** Some experts have suggested that the sample size should be **5%** of the population, while others have stated **10%**. Hence there is no hard and fast rule can be laid down that sample should be 5%, 10% or 25% of the universe size. The size alone may not ensure representativeness. A small sample may not represent the universe and the inferences may be mislead the researcher. A big size of sample is financial burden to the research project and also creates some problems. Hence the researcher should take a decision regarding the size of sample. The sample should be neither too small nor too large. The selected sample should be optimum size. An ideal size of ample should fulfil the requirements of efficiency, flexibility, reliability and representativeness. The ideal sample should be in proportion to universe. The funding position of the project also influences the size of sample. The degree of accuracy of the sample will depend upon the expert scientific approach. If the researcher wants to study intensively of a problem, it is better to select small sample.

Advantages and disadvantages of sampling

The sample is the representative of the universe. The procurement of sample is necessary for the smooth functioning of a research project. Sample is raw material for the researcher. The process of collecting a sample is known as **"sampling techniques"**. The sampling techniques have the following advantages over the population study.

(a) Short span of time
(b) Economy
(c) Reliable
(d) In-depth analysis
(e) Specified cases

(a) Short span of time

A universe can be studied with a sample. It is the representative of the whole. Sample survey provides less time and gives a scope for completion of project within short span of time. It provides samaller data in practice than a census. A lot of time and labour will be saved through efficient sampling techniques.

(b) Economy

Census method is an elaborative and costly affair for conducting a research. Sample survey reduces a lot of expenditure on the part of funding agency. It is useful for the underdeveloped countries to conduct research projects in less amount of expenditure. Collection of information is a costly affair in the research project. Hence sampling system provides a research project to complete with more economy aspect.

(c) Reliable

A researcher can procure his sample through sampling technique. Sampling techniques involve certain inaccuracies owing to sampling errors. The result obtained through sampling is more reliable than obtained from a census method. It is possible in sample method to take help from experts due to limited task in the problem area. The investigators may be imparted a thorough training which further reduces the possibility of errors. Experts are always helpful in the sample method because their task is limited to do a small part of work whereas in census method, they inclined to provide service.

(d) In-depth analysis

Sample means study of universe. A researcher can study a universe by selecting a small sample from the universe. It is possible in sampling method to study a problem in-depthly. An in-depth analysis may ensure to understand thoroughly the research problem by the researcher. Sampling method save a lot of time and labour.

(e) Specified cases

Census method is not always useful in all situations. Sample method is only practicable means in specified cases. If the population under investigation is infinite sampling is the only possible answer. Hence the researcher should keep in mind about the sampling techniques to select the sample for smooth completion of the research project.

Advantages

Sampling method is not always useful to the researcher. It has also some certain limitations. It is not completely free from limitations. In sample method, the researcher should always be careful. Otherwise the results may mislead the project. If sampling method is not properly followed, serious errors may arise. In this method, the expert's advice is highly useful to the researcher. If any absence of expert's advice may spoil the aim of the research project.

Sampling errors and non-sampling errors

Sample is the representative of the universe. For a meaningful survey, the sample must be most accurate. Sample is the raw material for the researcher. The quality of a product depends upon the input. An inferior quality of raw material may leads to produce substandard goods. Hence the quality of research project depends upon error free sampling. Generally errors are raised due to drawing inferences about the population as the basis of observation is called as **"sampling error"**. The errors in research study can be grouped as follows:

(a) Sampling errors
(b) Non-sampling errors

(a) Sampling errors

Sampling error means the error which arises in making inferences about the population as the basis of observations. Sampling error can be defined as "sampling error is the difference between the result of studying a sample and inferring a result about the population, and the result of the census of the whole population." — Patterson

Usually all researchers will take utmost care in selecting a sample. The obtained result from a sample study may not be exactly true in the population. Because the estimation is based on a past and not as a whole and samples are seldom, if ever, perfect miniature of the population. Therefore, sampling method of observation gives to certain errors known as **"sampling errors"**. However, these errors can be controlled and will be detected to a small extent. These errors are of two types:

(i) Biassed errors
(ii) Unbiassed errors

Biased errors may arise from selection of sample and estimation process. It is also known as cumulative or non-compensating error. **Bias** means a prejudice unfairly influencing treatment. The total sampling error is made up of errors due to bias. The bias forms a constant component of error that does not decrease in a large population as the number in the sample increases. Bias may arise in the following environment:

(a) Wrong process of selection
(b) Wrong collection process of sample
(c) Wrong methods of analysis

(a) Wrong process of selection: Sample is raw material for the research. Every researcher will take care about procurement of sample in a better method. A faulty selection of the sample may give chance to bias in many ways. Random selection of sample may give a chance of error. Sometimes substitution of an item in place of one chosen in random sample leads to bias. In same situations information supplied by the participants may also be biased.

(b) Wrong collection process of sample: Error may arise in collection of data. Usually all researchers will take utmost care in process of collection of data. Bias may arise due to improper formulation of the decision problem or wrongly defining the population, specifying wrong decision, securing an inadequate frame and so on. Biased observations may arise due to poor designing of questionnaire, untrained interviewers, failure or unwillingness of respondents memory etc.

(c) Wrong methods of analysis: Sometimes wrong method of analysis may cause to arise bias. Faulty methods of analysis may introduce bias. These kinds of bias can be avoided by adopting proper methods of analysis.

Sampling errors can be reduced by the researchers in several ways. The errors must be reduced to the minimum level to attain the desired accuracy. The errors can be reduced by increasing the sample size. It is easy way to increase the accuracy of sample than detection of error. The researcher has to take greater effect to decrease the sample error. After a certain stage to decrease the sampling error than in the initial instances.

(b) Non-sampling errors

Sample is a raw material for the researcher. The researcher will synthesise the data into a finished product. While converting the raw material into finished product, errors may arise in the process. Such errors are called as non-sampling errors. The process of tabulation may lead to arise non-sampling errors. They arise due to factors other than the inductive process of inferring about the population from a sample. Though the data contains error free from sampling method but it would be still be subject to non-sampling error. They occur at every stage of planning and execution of the survey. Most of the non-sampling errors arise due to lack of trained and experienced investigators, inadequate data, inappropriate statistical unit, inappropriate methods of interview, errors due to primary staff, errors due to non-response, errors in data processing operations, etc. These kinds of errors can be controlled by researcher in several ways. However, the samples reliability can be tested in many ways. The researcher should take more observations from the universe in order to reduce the errors. Hence it will be more reliable. Non-sampling errors include biases and mistakes. They occur at every stage of planning and execution of the survey. These errors arise due to a number of causes such as defective methods of data collection and tabulation, faulty definition, incomplete coverage of the population. They exist more in case of complete survey method than in case of a sample survey system.

3

SCALING TECHNIQUES

Introduction

Research means searching for an unknown fact. The universe is a combination of different elements. It is a reflection of many things known and unknown. The researcher is always trying to explore unknown things with the help of known facts. The utilisation of known things is known as experiment. Experiment needs a real factors generated from universe. The samples provide real factors to the researchers. The researchers should utilise these factors for qualitative or quantitative analysis of the study. The researcher has to measure the numerical aspects of the research problem. The collected samples should be measured with some yardstick to determine feature of a research object. Measurement is related to qualitative phenomenon. In research projects, measurement occupies a crucial role in the analysis of an observation. Measurement is the process of assigning numbers to objects or observations. Physical objectives can be measured like weight, height, and area etc. They can be measured directly with same standard units of measurement. For instance, measuring such things like intelligence, social status, marital adjustment and other things. Qualitative phenomenon like motivation, success, abilities, efficiency cannot be measured like physical properties. Inner feelings of the human relations can only be measured through scaling process. Measurement is a process to form of scale in the range and then transform the properties to the scale process. The measurement of qualitative phenomenon can be described with the help of scaling techniques. **For ex:** If a person's marital status we can record like 1, 2, 3 and 4 as the person is single, married, widowed and divorced. A researcher can also record **"Yes or No"** answers to a question as "O" and "I". A researcher may be involved either in qualitative or quantitative analysis to express his ideas more easily. Data can be made into numerical and assigns various codes for various categories of the information. Further discussion about data can be categorised as follows:

(a) Nominal data
(b) Ordinal data
(c) Interval data
(d) Ratio data

Nominal data means information contains numericals. They do not share any of the properties of the numbers. They express only in digits. They are associated with ordinary arithmetic. **For ex:** Recording of marital status 1, 2, 3 or 4 but cannot represent in arithmetical signs.

Ordinal data contains expression of information regarding inequalities of the research problem. It is useful when expression of qualitative factors regarding a particular aspect. **For ex:** We can compare the hardness of minerals such as talc, gypsum, calcium, fluorite, quartz, sapphire on the scale by assigning 1 to 10. From these codes we can express the hardness by giving code numbers to all minerals and can convey the message like **4 > 2** or **8 < 10**. Expressions regarding hardness of the material can be made comparing with fellow minerals with their designated code numbers. For a clear clarification, another example can be presented here for a thorough understanding of the ordinal data concept. **For ex:** All the states in India can be assigned as 1, 2, 3, 4, 5 .... and we can compare the states for prosperity, we can express in digits like greater than or less than method. Andhra Pradesh is assigned as 1, Punjab has been assigned 20. Therefore, we can say it **20 > 1**. Hence qualitative comparison can be made in this process.

Interval data is related to measure the properties of the objects or concepts. It reflects in setting up inequalities. It is useful in indication of temperature reading in degrees of Fahrenheit.

Ratio data is useful in expressing common measurement of objects. It is related to express the length, height, volume, area, pressure, monetary accounts, etc. It is associated with the traditional operations as mathematics.

All of the above methods of data expressions can be important for the nature of a set of data. It may suggest the use of particular statistical technique. Statistical data can be measured and they are interchangeable.

The data which are interchangeable is said to be **parametric tests**. These interchangeable aspects can be subjected to most kinds of statistical and mathematical processes. If the data is measured in units and are not interchangeable is said to be **"non-parametric"**.

Measurement scales in research operations

Measurement is related to qualitative and quantitative aspect of an object. It is associated with reflection of statistical data. Statistical data contains information with numerical. We can expect high accuracy in measurement of object. If the measurement tools are high standard then we will have more confident about the accuracy of the results of measurement. The scales of measurement can be considered in terms of the mathematical properties. The measurement of scales can be made as follows:

(A) Nominal Scale
(B) Ordinal Scale
(C) Interval Scale
(D) Ratio Scale

(A) Nominal scale

Nominal scale is an ordinary system of measurement of the data. It is a simple system. It is the least powerful measurement tool. It has no arithmetic origin. There is no order between things. It is very useful and widely used in research surveys. It simply exposes differences between things by assigning them to categories. It provides best ways of keeping track of people, objects and aspects. It is the process of assignment of numbers to different things. The assigned numbers are only just for convenient and has no quantitative value. The assigned numbers are not based as real value of the content. They contains only serial order to measure the degree of scale. It can be employed for conducting chi-square test, measures of correlation, contingency table etc.

(B) Ordinal scale

Ordinal scale is associated with the ranking of events from highest to lowest. It is based on the measurement of ranks. It is the lowest level of ordered scale. Ranking method is frequently used in research works. Research works, which are related to qualitative aspect of study, would utilise this measurement of scale. It cannot be used for more precise comparisons. Ordinal scale uses the appropriate measure of central tendency is **"median"**. Median is one of the average which is based on positional arrangement. A percentile quartile deviations are used in measurement of dispersion. All these methods are related to the **"Non-parametric tests"**. Ordinal scale does not expose the different between ranks. **For ex:** The actual difference between rank 1 and 2 may be more or less than difference between ranks 9 and 10.

(C) Interval scale

Interval scale is a powerful measurement than other scales. It is the more powerful tool in the hands of researcher for statistical measures. Arithmetic mean is a good tool for measuring central tendency of data standard deviation is widely used measure of dispersion. The researcher can use tools like **"correlation, E test, F test"** for his investigation of the experiment. It incorporates the concept of equality of interval. **For ex:** We can say that an increase in temperature from 25° to 35° involves the same increase in temperature as an increase from 50° to 70°. But we cannot say that the temperature of **70°** is twice as warm as the temperature of 35°.

(D) Ratio scale

Ratio scale is useful for making comparison between two variables. It is more useful to research in physical sciences. It represents the actual amounts of variables. It measures physical dimensions such as weight, height, distances, etc. It uses all statistical techniques in research work. All manipulations can be carried out with ratio scale value. In this scale, multiplication and division can also be used, but in other scales, is not possible. It has an absolute or true zero of measurement. **For ex:** An unabsolute temperature is theoretically unobtainable and it remains in the researcher's mind. In this scale we can reflect the number of errors in a typed pages. The violation of minor traffic rules can also be monitored through this scale. Geometric and harmonic means are measured for central tendency and co-efficient of variations also be calculated. It is the most precise scale.

It is not useful to behavioural sciences research work. The performance of two skilled persons can be observed in this scale.

Research is a process of knowing factor from facts. Measurement reveals the accuracy of numericals collected and processed by the researcher. The collected variables can be measured in physical dimensions such as weight, height and distance. Statistical tools techniques are utilised with ratio scales and all manipulations will be carried out by the analyst. Geometric and harmonic means may be used of measuring central tendency. Coefficient of variations can also be calculated. From all the available scales the researcher should choose the scale that provides the most useful to his research theme. The nominal scale provides the least precise type of scale. The ratio scale reveal the most precise type of information to the observer. Researcher belonging to physical sciences will use to describe variables in **"Ratio scale"**. The social sciences researchers are usually limited to describe variables in **"Interval scale form"**. Interval scale is a less precise type of measurement. A good research study should have accurate data and there should not be scope for any kind of errors. This objective will not be materialised due to certain limitations. Hence the researcher should be in a position to find out the sources of errors in measurement. Generally the following are the sources of possible errors in measurement while conducting a research project.

(i) Respondent
(ii) Time
(iii) Interviewer
(iv) Method

(i) Respondent

Generally all research projects are conducted as per the objectives. The objectives of the study requires to conduct the interviews, surveys from the targeted audiences. The targeted persons provide first hand information about the specific problem. They are known as **"Respondents"**. Respondents provide an important information that reflects thc study. Sometimes respondents may be reluctant to express their negative feelings or they may have very little knowledge about the subject. Sometimes they will give answers on guessing situation. In some situations, the respondents are not interested to reveal about their financial information such as yearly investment, yearly earnings, yearly tax payment, etc. Hence the objective of the study may not be fulfilled while the respondents are reluctant to provide actual information. In some situations transient factors may curtail the ability of the respondent to provide accurate information.

(ii) Time

The information will be collected from the field by the investigators. The investigators will serve or present the questionnaire to the respondent. The respondents are required to give their explanation or reply to the survey or schedule. The interviewer research the respondent proximity and asks questions about the research subject. The length of interview time is also one of the most influential factor in delivering the answers. A time consumed interview may place a strain as interview can have serious effects as rapport between interviewer and respondent. Sometimes other persons may join in between respondent and interviewer. The respondents may not be able to spend much time and the answers will be given in a hurry situation.

(iii) Interviewer

Interviewer or investigator is the most important person in collection of information from the field. The accurate and first hand information will be collected by him. The behaviour of the interviewer will show impact on the study. The interview should be in a friendly atmosphere but not like an interrogation. The questioning method, style, courtesy and hospitality of the interviewer will show impact on the study. Sometimes interviewer can distort answers by repeating questions. Sometimes interviewer may commit mistakes or errors due to incorrect coding, faulty tabulation, or in data analysis.

(iv) Method

A quick completion of research will depend upon the best methodology adopted by the researcher. Researcher should choose a best non-defective instrument to carry out the research programme. He should also think about the errors arises during the implementation of the research method. Research method is an instrument which is helpful in smooth functioning of the research work process. Generally errors may arise due to defective measuring instruments, used by the researcher in pursuing of the study. Errors may arise in pursuance of research project like poor printing, usage of words, terminology, inadequate space for explanation, respondent choice, etc. Sometimes errors may arise due to poor sampling of the universe items.

Hence, the researcher should take care all about the errors, which may arise in conducting the research work operations process. He should try to minimise the errors and take all precautions before commencement of research project work. Error free findings may stimulate the value of research results. An accurate measurement of data produces error free results. Error free results meet all the tests of **validity, reliability and practicality**. All these tests are known as measurement tools. They are useful in evaluating a research project. Validity provides authenticity to a research finding. Reliability deals with the accuracy and precision of a measurement procedure. Another important factor practicality is related to a wide range of elements such as convenience, budget and flexibility. Hence it is more important to discuss briefly about these tests. They are:

(A) Test of Validity
(B) Test of Reliability
(C) Test of Practicality

(A) Test of Validity: Validity is one of the ingredient to evaluate the research findings. It indicates the usefulness of the research work. It specifies about the utility of the findings. It reveals about the true differences among those being tested. Validity can be categorised in two kinds: **(a) External validity, (b) Internal validity**. External validity deals with generalisation of findings to population or universe. Adoptability or acceptability to universe is known as external validity. Internal validity means, a measurement of research findings with related objectives of the study. It evaluates, how far the researcher succeeded in pursuance of his study. In this situation, validity can be divided into **three types**: (a) content validity, (b) criteria validity, (c) construct validity. **Content validity** is related to measure the adequate coverage of the topic under study. Coverage of research topic is one of the most important factor in evaluating a research project. The content of the topic should be balance and it should not be over or under emphasised. A good research project contains a representative sample of the universe. The content validity cannot be expressed in numerical way. It is a qualitative phenomenon. The standard of the content depends upon the right instrument. Content validity can also be determined by a panel of experts. **Criteria validity** is another test of validity. It reveals further process of investigation of the research study. It reflects the existence of current situation. It reflects the success of measures for empirical investigation. It possess same characteristics like **"Relevance, reliability and freedom"**. **Construct validity** deals with the accuracy of measurement of numerical information. It compares results of the research work with others work. It predicts correlations with other theoretical propositions.

(B) Test of Reliability: Test of reliability is one of the tests of measurement. It provides validity for the research work. Validity occupies an important value in assessment. Reliability is not as valuable as validity. Reliability can be studied in two dimensions, i.e., **stability and equivalence**. Stability is related to a strong consistent secured results pursued by a same research scholar with repeated experiments. The stability aspect is depended upon the results of repeated measurements. **Equivalence** aspect require measurement of experiment's results by different investigators for the same event. The same study will be carried out by different research scholars and their observations will be compared and analysed. However, reliability can be maximised through by avoiding of external factors such as boredom and fatigue. The stability aspect will be enhanced by using trained and strongly committed people. A highly motivated research personnel can definitely stimulate the stability aspect.

(C) Test of Practicality: Research means exploring new avenues for providing better facilities to a layman. Any kind of research work carried out by any researcher should be useful to the society. Exploring new avenues to make sophisticated life to the layman. Hence the research work should always be useful to the society otherwise it will be wasteful and costly exercise. The research work can be judged through measuring in terms of economy, flexibility and interpretability. **Budget** is an important economic aspect for commencing a project. The sponsored agency will take into consideration of monetary aspects. Usually the observation time or interview time will greatly show impact on study. The mode of data collection may greatly influence the cost of research project. At present research studies can be pursued through modern communication methods like **"e-mail,**

cellular phones, fax" etc. Alternatives for smooth functioning of research work. All these aspects depend upon economic aspects. **Flexibility** is another important measuring instrument for pursuing research study. The measuring instrument should be ideal and easy to administer. For conducting an interview method of observation, a good designed questionnaire will greatly show more effective and complete the work within a period of short time.

Techniques

Research is a continuous process in society. It will not be limited for a specific period. It provides better solutions to the society's problems. It saves millions of lives in medical field. Research in medical and life sciences can change life style of a layman. A continuous research in cancer disease found solutions for treatment. Once upon a time **"T.B."** is most dangerous disease and there is no chance for treatment. But at present it is a simple disease just like as a **Fever and Headache**. After a lot of continuous efforts made by scientists new tools of measuring techniques available to the community. The development of measuring tools arises in four stages. They are presented below:

(a) Formation of concept
(b) Development of concept
(c) Measurement of concept
(d) Index

(a) Formation of idea generation is the first and basic step for shaping a research design. A motivated researcher always thinks about to provide a better solution to the society through his research experiment. In this situation an idea will generate in his brain and tries to understand the major concepts pertaining to his study. Idea generation is the most important step in pursue of research problem.

(b) Concept development is another important task before the researcher. The researcher should have a thorough understanding about the problem of the study. He must have full confidence on the related subject. He is the guiding force to upcoming researchers. He may became a model social scientist to the future researchers. Hence the researcher should take more carefulness in developing the concept.

(c) Measurement of concept occupies an important role in determining the research project work. The researcher shall specify the various dimensions of the problem. He must analyse problem in different ways in order to provide a good solution to the community. This task may either be accomplished by reduction. The researcher may either increase or reduce keeping in view of the degree of problem. The researcher should develop indicators for measuring each component of the project. Generally every researcher will take care about questions, scales to be adopted and other devices. All these indicators can be utilised by the respondent's knowledge, opinion, expectation and perception. Hence all precautions should be taken by the researcher after examining several alternatives. The perfect use of select indicators will enhance the value of study. Indicators provide more stability to the scores and improves the quality of work for validity.

(d) Index is the final step for completion of several combined indicators performance result. If the study has several dimensions of a concept, then they will be combined into a single index. Overall index can be arrived with summing up of responding scores. It provides a good measurement tool to assess the research work. **Scaling** is an important factor in research work to know the opinion or expression from the targeted audience. It is a process for collection of information. It assigns numbers to various degrees of opinions, feelings, expressions, attitude and other concepts. The researcher will face problems while measuring through scaling process. Measuring the opinion through scaling technique can be done in through two ways: **(a)** In this way the individual characteristics will be placed directly as a sale that has been defined in terms of that characteristics. **(b)** In this method, a questionnaire will be prepared to assess the opinion or expression of an individual as the scale. A scale will be prepared consisting of highest points and lowest points along with other factors between these points. The scale will be prepared keeping in view of an individual's preference, favourableness etc. The scale points will depend upon each factor or on priority basis of the individual. Scaling is applied to the procedures for attempting to determine the quantitative aspects of the subject abstract concepts scaling means, a procedure for assigning numbers to a property of objects related to a subjective questions. Scaling procedure can be broadly classified as follows:

(i) Subject Orientation
(ii) Analytical Orientation

(iii) Personal Preference Orientation
(iv) Scale Properties
(v) Multiple Factors Orientation

(i) Subject orientation

Research means exploring or testing about a particular aspect of a related problem. The study of measure of performance or opinion or expression may be collected from the respondents through a wide range of questions. In this method of investigation scale may be designed to measure or assess the characteristics of the respondents. Respondents provide a first hand information about a particular aspect or satisfaction for a purchased branch of a product. They clearly provide full information regarding a branded product or services. They will provide a spontaneous information about quality of a product or services. They are able to judge the quality of a product or services.

(ii) Analytical orientation

In this method, the scale may be categorised as **"categorical and comparative"**. Categorical scale can also be called as rating scale. In this scale, a respondent scores same object without direct reference to other objects. In comparative scale, the respondent will be asked to compare two or more objects. This comparative scale is also known as **"Ranking scale"**. Ranking scale provides a clear information regarding preference of a particular object. The respondent will be asked to show one object which is superior to other objects. We can collect the information regarding a particular object as per the priority of the respondent. They will be asked to assign ranks as 1, 2, or 3. In this method, a comparison between different objects will be studied. At one moment, we can learn more things about the determined objects. A relative comparison is possible in this method of scaling process.

(iii) Personal preference orientation

In this method of scaling process, the expression or opinion or tastes of preference regarding a particular object can be measured. The respondents are asked to state their personal preferences or simply make non-preference judgements. They will be questioned to select a particular object as per their wishes. Sometimes they will have to choose the object without reflecting any personal preferences. Hence it is one of the scaling method to measure the subjective personal preferences.

(iv) Scale properties

Research is a tool to explore many new things. The new things are not found suddenly in the universe. These things are new for us. These things are known by us. Research will be helpful to find out these things which are hidden in the nature. Man is exploring all these things from the universe. He will procure the information scientifically and data will be measured accurately. Data can be measured through different scales such as **Nominal, Ordinal, Interval** and **Ratio**. In nominal scale method, the data will be provided to the respondent without any order or distance. The ordinal scale is related to study about the particular object is **"less than"** or **"more than"** method. The information will be more meaningfully analysed with less or more method way of presentation. It enables the reader more interest in findings. The tastes or attitude of the respondents for a particular property of an object. **Interval scales** have a combination of order preference and distance values. It is a combination of both aspects of the preference and distance.

(v) Multiple Factors orientation

In this method of measurement of data, scales can be divided into two methods, i.e., **Undimensional** and **Multidimensional**. In the first method, the researcher can measure only one object of the study. In multi-dimensional method, the research can measure an object in more dimensions rather than a single aspect. Hence the researcher can measure in different ways of aspects, as he wishes.

Research is a weapon to counter the poverty. Research will be more useful to a nation to stabilise technologically. Technology is a highly influential factor in development. The modern technology can make layman's life more comfortable and sophisticated. The study of measuring data regarding a research problem depends upon its scaling process. Scaling is more important factor in extraction of information from respondents. The scales should be constructed more meaningfully in order to find out accurate results. There are five methods of techniques to construct scale operations.

(a) Ad hoc basis
(b) Consensus basis
(c) Factors basis
(d) Cumulative analysis
(e) Inter-correlation basis

Ad hoc basis is also known as "**Arbitrary approach**". It is most popular approach. It is used by many research scholars in different studies. It is developed as ad hoc basis. It measures the concept of a research problem.

Consensus approach is one of the techniques of construction of a scale. The scale will be constructed with help of panel of experts. The experts will evaluate the items selected for incorporating in the measurement instrument. They will examine whether these items are relevant to topic area or any diversion of subject. They will reduce any ambiguous in research process.

Factor approach is another important technique in construction of a scale. In this method, individual items are tested. All the questions consisting like a test will be served to all respondents. Respondents are asked to express their opinion regarding research area of problems. The total scores of all the respondents will be calculated individually. Individual items will be analysed to determine the results. The researcher can find out the high total scores and with low scores.

Cumulative analysis method of scale provides ranking position to a research object. It chooses the items based on ranking of items with ascending and descending order. In this method the researcher will provide higher position for endorsement of a particular object and lower position to another objects. Hence there will be a discriminating power at the disposal of researcher's hands.

Inter-correlation basis is also known as factor scale approach. It may be constructed on the basis of relation between research items. It measures the relation about a common factor between various items.

Scaling Techniques in Business Research or Social Sciences

Social sciences deals with the attitude and movement of a human being in society. Society is a group of combination of different castes, religious persons. Social scientist will observe all the changes which are happening in and around society. Business research is more important to the corporate world, where it is completely neglected at present. The performance of a business enterprise depends upon the prediction capabilities. Prediction is most influential factor in stabilisation of a business enterprise. Prediction is always depends upon past. Past is the indicator of the future trend. Trend is an element which reflects the market movement. Market movement reveals the supply and demand position along with price fluctuations. Acquiring market information provide for taking a good business decision. A research based decision will definitely stimulate the profitability of the corporate sector. Profit is the barometer for measuring the efficiency of a business concern. For increasing the business firm's efficiency, the businessman must have research based findings. Therefore important scaling techniques often used in business or in social sciences are presented below for thorough understanding of the problem.

(a) Rating scales
(b) Arbitrary scale
(c) Differential scale
(d) Likert type scale
(e) Factor scales
(f) Multi-dimensional scales

Rating scale is one of the important techniques for measuring properties of a research object. It is related to qualitative aspects of the description of a research object. It is providing an opportunity for greater sensitivity of measuring object. It may be either a graphic rating scale or an itemised rating scale. It is involved to measure a limited number of aspects of thing of a person. Personal opinion or expression can be extracted through this kind of scale. It measures the properties of objects without reference to other similar objects. These ratings are useful to know the qualitative aspects of the object. Rating scale may be in such forms as **"average, above average, below average"** or **"like, dislike"** or **"excellent, good, average, below average, poor"** or **"like very much, like, neutral, dislike, dislike very much"** etc. In this kind of measurement, the researcher can measure through a two point or three point scale or scale with more points. Hence there is no specific rule about taking a number of points rating scale for measuring a research object. Generally all researchers will use **3 to 7** points scales to measure a research object. These scales may further be categorised as follows:

(a) Graphic rating scale
(b) Itemised rating scale

Graphic rating scale is a simple measurement of a process. It is widely used in many research project. In this method, the answer will be placed as a line and the respondent is asked to indicate his rating by simply making a tick mark **(✓)** at the appropriate term. All explanations to the question may be presented in a straight line and the rating process will be done more easily. The following illustration will reveal clearly about the rating process:

How do you like hospitality service in a Star hotel

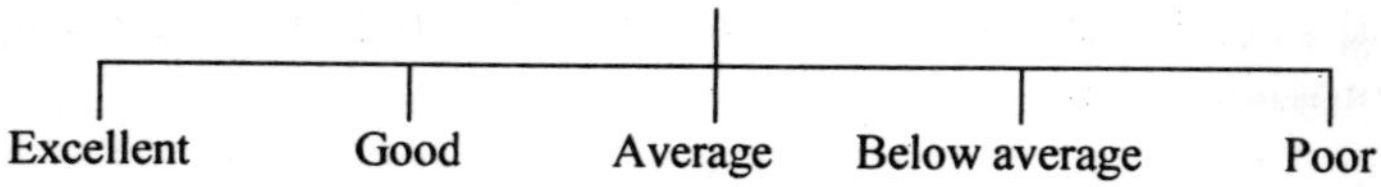

The respondent is asked to simply check the (✓) mark at appropriate answer. This method of scaling has several limitations. The researcher can use other scales to measure the personal traits of an object. The respondents have choice to select an appropriate answer for their questions administered by the researcher. The meanings of the terms like **"Excellent, Good"** may depend upon the respondents choice. The researcher can assess the satisfactory levels of the respondent.

The itemised rating scale is also called as **Numerical Scale.** Numerical rating scale provides a best reflections of respondents opinions regarding a research problem. The statements are prepared to evaluate the respondents feelings regarding a specified object. It is more useful in analysis of qualitative aspects of the object. The personal behaviour or social relations of a targeted person's can be assessed or observed. It provides more meaningful information to the rater. It increases reliability of the value of information procured from this process. Rating scales are useful to extract the information from the respondents with more clarity and accurate findings. The scales are useful to compare favourably with various methods alternatives. Scales require less time of processing information and provide a wide range of applications.

The rating scale may provide for study a large number of properties or variables. The accuracy of the observed result depends upon the careful collection of information by the researcher from the respondents. If the respondents are not very careful, there will be a scope for errors. Errors can be classified in three kinds **"error of leniency, central tendency, hallo"**. **Error of leniency** means some respondents may easy raters and same other hard raters. This error arises in certain situations. It depends upon the behaviour of respondent. The respondents should be more cautious while assessing the feelings or opinions of the audience. The measurement purpose depends upon the assumptions and the respondents can take good judgement decisions. **The error of central tendency** occurs when raters are reluctant to provide better judgment. **The errors hallo effect** is related to change from one rating scale to another. It occurs over a generalised impression of the subject. This kind of error arise in conclusion of a report. It is likely to occur when a respondent asked many factors in a given scale.

Ranking scales is also called as **"Comparative scale"**. In this method researcher can compare two or more objects and make better choice among them. This scale further can be categorised into two ways:

(a) Paired comparison
(b) Rank order

Paired comparison is associated with comparison of two products or brands. In this method, the respondent can express his opinion by making a choice or selection between two products. It is useful to narrate the brand qualities of a product. A respondent can make a choice for a new flavour of coffee and established brand of coffee. If the respondent has to judge more than two brands, the comparison should be made by the following formula:

$$N = \frac{n(n-1)}{2}$$

N = Number of judgements
n = number of objects to be judged

In this method, if the number of judgements happens to be more, there will be risk in getting explanation from respondents or they may even refuse to answer. Hence the investigator should take care about a small number of judgments. It is easy to get the better findings by reducing the number of comparisons for making research study for more useful. We can reduce the number of comparisons by choosing a few objects covering with equal intervals and comparing all other objects paired comparison provides general data, but the same will be converted into an interval scale by the law of comparative judgement. This judgement was developed by **L.L. Thurstons**. It involves the conversion of frequencies of preferences into a table of proportions.

Rank order is another method to collect the information from respondents. The respondents are asked to rank their choices. It is very easy process to rank their comparisons. It is faster than the method of paired comparisons. **For ex:** If a researcher wants to_compare 40 pairs, simply he can ask the respondents rank top 10 items only. The researcher can also ask the respondents to rank all 40 items as per choice.

Construction techniques

Social science is a study of human behaviour in society. It deals with the different attitudes of the people belonging to different nations, different religions, different castes and different communities. Universe is a combination of different people. The attitude of people depends upon their culture, traditions, belief, sentiments and feelings. The attitude can be measured through the technique of preparing the **"opinionnaire"**. Opinionnaire is an information that attempts to measure the attitude or belief of an individual. It is also known as **"attitude scale"**. The individual responses from the respondents will be placed as a scale. The respondent can express his opinion either agreement or disagreement with a number of statements relevant to the issue. In this method, the psychological factors can only be measured. The statements will elicit responses relevant to the psycho factors of the people. Therefore, psychologists and sociologists have developed several methods of rating techniques for research purpose. The researcher should have knowledge about the uses of these different techniques. Generally the following approaches exist in social science research programmes:

(A) Arbitrary scales

(B) Differential scales
(C) Summated scales
(D) Cumulative scales
(E) Factor scales
(G) Multi-dimensional scales

Arbitrary scales are designed on ad hoc basis. They are related to study the attitude of respondents. The researcher can incorporate his own subjective selection of items. He may ask the respondents with a list of several statements for measuring the attitude and belief of the public for his research work. These scales can be developed very easily, quickly and with low expenses. These scales are widely used in practice. These scales have same limitations. These scales can also be prepared with higher specific needs of the researcher. However, the researcher's competency, proficiency and efficiency can be found in the research programme.

Differential scales are also known as **"Thurstone"** type scale. It can be called as **consensus** scale approach. In this approach, the required information will be assessed by a panel of experts. The experts will decide the selection of items to be collected through this technique. The panel of judges will evaluate items in terms of relevant to the topic area of research. The following diagram will indicate the process of research work:

Preparation of 20 statements related to research topic	Stage I
↓	
Submission of 20 statements to the panel of Judges	Stage II
↓	
Evaluation of the statements by Judges—additions or deletions	Stage III
↓	
Assigning of median position to the statements as per Judge's view	Stage IV
↓	
Final selection of statement made by panel of Judge to administer to respondents	Stage V

The above diagram will reveal about the process of selection of statements with the advice of panel of judges. The selected statements will be administered to the respondents by the researcher. The respondents are asked to indicate their opinions or expressions or feelings. The statements are arranged in random order of scale value. The questionnaire appears to tap a different attitudes of the respondents. This method has been used widely to measure the attitude towards typical issues like war and religion.

Summated scales are associated with the observation of a favourable or unfavourable attitudes of the respondents. It is also known as **Likert type scale**. It is developed by using the item analysis approach. It consists a number of statements to get the respondent's attitude. The respondent will react to the statements, which are served by the researcher. The respondent will indicate his agreement or disagreement for each statement in the questionnaire. Every response will be assigned with a numerical score, indicating its favourableness or unfavourableness. The scores will be totalled and respondent's attitudes will be found. Hence the overall score represents the respondent's attitude towards research programme. These scales are mostly used in the study of social attitudes. This pattern was developed by **Likert**. It is mostly used in measurement of job satisfaction of employers, workers and labourers. **For ex:** For evaluation of job perception, about pleasant working environment, the respondent may indicate his expression in the following ways:

(1) Strongly agree
(2) Agree
(3) Undecided
(4) Disagree
(5) Strongly disagree

The respondent has to select just his opinion regarding statements. **For ex:** A researcher, who served the questionnaire with **25** statements, the following score values would be as follows:

$25 \times 5 = 125$ **Most favourable attitude**
$25 \times 3 = 75$ **A undecided attitude**
$25 \times 1 = 25$ **Most unfavourable attitude**

The score would fall between 25 and 125 for individual. The process of construction of this scale can be presented in the following table.

Collection of large number of statements by the researcher	Step I
↓	
Trial test will be conducted with a small group of people	Step II
↓	
Assigning of numerical value for statements most favourable most unfavourable	Step III
↓	
Totalling of all statements scores	Step IV
↓	
Arrival of highest and lowest scores	Step V

This method of scale has several advantages. It is very easy method to construct the scale. It can be processed and executed without help of a panel of judges. It does not require experts interference in the research project. It provides full freedom to the researcher in execution of his research project. It is more reliable process. It provides more information and data about the research project. It gathers plenty of information from the respondents. An in-depth analytical questions will be framed by the researcher. The respondents are free in selection of their answers. Each statement or question is given an empirical test will be conducted for results. It takes less time to construct. This method has also several **limitations**. In this method it is not possible to measure the satisfactory levels of the respondents. Each and every statement is provided with five answers like "strongly agree", "agree" may not spell equal expression of the respondents. It does not expose actual opinion or expressions of the respondent's as overall statements. It provides a little clear meaning only. It gathers more information but generate results with little amount of expressions.

Cumulative scales are related to gather information from the respondents regarding a particular aspect about expressing his agreement or disagreement. It is also known as **"Louis Gutman"** analysis. It consists a series of statements and collect the opinion from the respondents. A number of series of statements will be served to the respondents to get his expression from the well-designed and planned information. In this method, the statements are related to one another. The respondent has to say favourable or unfavourable to a specified statements. The statements are interlinked with each other. If the respondent expressed his opinion regarding favourable position to statement No. **5**, he has to say favourable from question

Nos. 1, 2, 3, 4. The answers are reflection of cumulative basis situations. The individual attitude will be measured as favourable items on one side and unfavourable score on another side. The respondents attitude will be measured through counting of favourable and unfavourable responses of the statements. On arrival of total score, we can estimate the respondent's satisfaction level on this scale. This technique developed by **"Louis Gutman"**. It is termed as **"scalogram"** analysis. It further called as **"scale analysis"**. In this method the expression of the respondent's feelings can be measured as follows:

Response Analysis

Statements Number				*Respondent Score*
4	3	2	1	
—	—	—	—	0
—	—	—	X	1
—	—	X	X	2
—	X	X	X	3
X	X	X	X	4

X = Agree — = Disagree

The respondents are asked to answer the statements freely. A score of **4** numerical number reveal that respondent is in agreement with all the statements. It indicates most favourable attitude of the respondent. But the score 3 reveals that the respondent is not favourable to statement No. **4**, but he is favourable to item numbers 1, 2 and 3. In the same process we can prepare his expressions or can measure the respondent's satisfactory levels. The following table will indicate the process of scalogram analysis.

Framing of clear terms regarding research study	Step I
↓	
Fixing of number of items to be asked to the respondents	Step II
↓	
Pre-testing the items to determine the size of issue	Step III
↓	
Final Phase—Respondents are asked to record their opinion on items	Step IV

Scalogram analysis requires pre-testing the items to determine the size of opinionnaire. In pre-testing stage the items may include 12 statements. The final scale may have only **4 to 6** items. In the pretext stage the opinionnaires are served to **25** members. But in final stage of operation and execution, it should be served to **100** or more. In the pretext stage the respondents are asked to record their opinion as 5 point rating scale. Final test results may be tabulated and analysis will be made.

Factor scales are related to study on the basis of intercorrelations between items of the statements. It is based on factor analysis. This analysis is useful for uncovering latent attitude dimensions. It can be categorised into two ways: **(1) Semantic Differential (2) Multidimensional scaling. Semantic scale** developed by **Charles Osgood, G.J. Suci and P.H. Tannebum** in 1957. It is based on same assumptions. As per this approach every object can have varied dimensions. It consists 7 points scale by which are or more respondents rate one or more concepts on each scale item. The psychological feelings can be measured for determining leadership capabilities of a person. The following diagram will illustrate the process of semantic scaling technique.

Selection of concepts of the study	Stage I
↓	
Selection of scale across subjects and concepts	Stage II
↓	
Panel of Judges determine the composite scaling	Stage III

It has a number of specified advantages. It is more useful to get respondents feelings from a large sample. These attitudes can be measured with the help of statistical tools. The statistical tools has the power to measure the intensity and directions of the psychological feelings.

Multi-dimensional is one of the factor scale method. It can measure the object with a minimum sources of information. It is used in all study of variables. It can be used in metric and non-metric study methods. It is useful to study all the variables which are happen to be independent. People perceive a set of objects indifferent dimensions for the same variable. As per the metric approach, the solution will be provided with the help of the full information. The information provides plenty of data regarding numerical information.

If the true and real data is not available, then the solution can be obtained through random and systematic procedures. **The non-metric** approach procure the information by asking respondents to rank all pairs.

Multi-dimensional scaling is a combination of metric and non-metric approach. This scale is more useful to psychologists to measure the respondents satisfaction towards several brands. It is an important tool in measurement of attitudes of the respondents. It is easy to measure the company images, advertisement brands, etc. It is not widely practised by the social scientists due to computational complications. These methods are more laborious in terms of collection of data and tabulation process. At present it is widely using in market research area of functional management. It is useful in getting the results regarding product pricing, consumer behaviours, spending patterns of the public etc. The future is very bright in behaviour sciences due to heavy rushes in formation and expansion of the corporate sector.

4

COLLECTION OF DATA

Introduction

Research means exploring new sources of information from universe. Unexposed facts can be found through research. Research provides a basic solution to the existing problem. It should be able to provide remedy for the problems faced by the society. Society problems should be solved by a good research theme. A wonderful research theme is a weapon to counter the problems faced by community. A research theme will be constructed by the researcher with a planned, scientific and careful analysis of the object. A good research theme contains full of numerical information. A combination of different kinds of numerical information is called **"Data"**. Data consists of full information regarding a particular aspect. The procurement of numerical information from a different sources of information for a single object is known as **"collection of data"**. The research theme indicates about the collection of data which depends upon the objectives of the study. The main objective is the lifeblood of a research project for finding solutions to the community problem. The well-planned research design determine the flow of data to be collected, analysed for the society. The collection of data starts from plans prepared by the researcher. After finalisation of research design, the methodology indicates further investigations to complete the research project. However, the researcher should keep in mind about the procurement of data from the available sources of information. Generally the data can be classified as:

(a) Primary data
(b) Secondary data

(a) Primary Data

Data contains numerical information. Information is the most powerful device at the disposal of the social scientists. Data expresses a number of ways of meanings for a single aspect. Data speaks many things. Data occupies an important ingredient in quantitative analysis of the research studies. Primary data means collection of information at the first time for the research study. It is original in nature. It is procured for a particular research aspect. This data can be used only for this research project. It is collected by the researcher through is investigators or his team members from respondents. The researcher should select his methods to procure the data from the field. He will prepare plans to execute the research work through a different set of tasks. The researcher will collect primary data in execution of his experiments. Experiment is an investigation to explore the fact under a test. It is an examination of a truth under different variables. In case of descriptive type research, the researcher can undertake through sample survey or census survey methods. Then the researcher can decide for further work to get the information either through **observation or interview method**. The required information can be elicited by the researcher as per the procedure stipulate the situation. **Survey** is another method to collect information from the selected respondents from the concerned universe. There are several methods of collecting primary data for conducting research projects. They are presented below:

(a) Observation method
(b) Interview method
(c) Questionnaire method
(d) Schedules method
(e) Miscellaneous methods

(a) Observation method

Observation method is widely popular method in collection of primary data. In case of surveys and descriptive research, primary data is more useful to draw findings and inferences. It is most commonly used in behavioural sciences studies. In day to day activities of a layman, he may observe many things happening around him, but it may not be a scientific observation. Observation will become a scientific tool, when it prepared and planned scientifically. A scientific method of observation can yield accurate findings and conclusions. A well planned, careful and thoughtfully selected method of data collection serves a research purpose. It is systematically planned and recorded for various checks for validity and reliability. In this method, the researcher will appoint some investigators to elicit information from the respondents. The investigators will get the information from the respondents without asking them anything. The investigator will observe what kind of brand used by a person without asking any question. By observation method, we can avoid subjective bias. Observations yield accurate results. It provides current information. It does not reveal past and future. It is only limited to explore present environment of the situation. In this method, the respondent's cooperation is not necessary for the completion of data records. Simply, the investigator can finish the work by observing the feelings of the respondents. This method is more useful to elicit information from **illiterate respondents**. However, it has also several limitations. It is an expensive method of collection of information. It provides little amount of information. There is possibility to arise unforeseen situation while observing the feelings of the respondents. Sometimes, it may not be possible to access the respondents to observe feelings. The researcher should use this method more carefully. It is not possible to use this method of collection of information from respondents in any situation. The researcher should keep in mind, important things to observe feelings, recording method of observation, units of observation, accuracy of observation. Observation means watching carefully everything. Observation can be divided into two kinds **(a) structured observation, (b) unstructured observation. Structured** observation means, a careful standardised unit of information to be observed. The standardised conditions of observation, the selection of pertinent data observation can be termed as structured observation. **Unstructured** observation means gathering of information without any standardised units. These observations can be made without any planning or in advance. **Structured observation** is suitable for descriptive research studies. Unstructured observation method is found to be appropriate in **exploratory studies**.

Observation method further can be divided into two methods **(a) Participant, (b) Non-participant method**. These two methods are more popular in social science research. **Participant observation** means the observer is a member of group and he is sharing experiences about the life of the group. As a member of the group, he knows everything and every aspect and making his observations in his own way. **Non-participant observation** means the observer records the feelings of the respondents without any participation in the group as a member. Sometimes, the observer records the feelings of others without knowing his identity. Hence this method of observation is known as **disguised observation**. Participant observation provides an opportunity to record the natural behaviour of the group. In this method, the observer can observe real feelings of the group members. He can find out hidden facts which are lying in their hearts. The researcher can verify the facts of the statement. It has also some limitations in procuring information from the respondents. The observation method is related to psychological factor and the observer may loose emotional feelings while recording the feelings of the respondents.

Observation method can also be categorised as **Controlled and Uncontrolled. Controlled observation** means recording of feelings as per pre-arranged plans by the observer. It involves an experimental procedure. **Uncontrolled** observation takes place naturally. It provides a real picture of life and persons. It does not require any plan to record the feeling. It provides natural and complete behaviour of the human being. It provides sufficient time to capture the real feelings. However, controlled observation requires mechanical instruments to measure the accuracy and standardisation of the information. Controlled observations are carried out in laboratory experiments. Uncontrolled observation can be applied for **exploratory researches**.

(b) Interview Method

Primary data can be collected through interview method. It is one of the process of collection of information. It involves presentation of oral communication. The researcher can gather information through exchange of information. The respondents are being asked to different aspects of the contents. It is widely used practice in collection of information in social sciences. Interviews can be classified into two kinds:

(A) Personal Interview
(B) Telephonic Interview

(A) Personal Interview: Personal interview method is one of the sources of collection of information. The respondents are asked orally by the researcher or the investigator. It is a face to face contact relation between interviewer and respondents. Interviewer will take initiative for starting an interview process. A person who is asking questions is called as **Interviewer**. He will get information from the respondents. Interviews may be conducted either in **direct personal investigation** or **indirect oral examination** method. In the direct personal investigation method, the interviewer has to collect the information directly speaking with respondents. He will get information on the spot and very easy to collect the information from the concerned people. It is more useful for intensive investigations. The researcher should be remembered that direct collection of information may not be possible at all situations. In such cases researcher can use indirect oral examinations to collect the required information from concerned people. This method is also useful to cross check the information and facts may be recorded. Interviews can be further categorised as **structured interview and unstructured interview**. Structured interview means, a method of collection of information with the use of a set of pre-determined questions. This method involves highly standardised techniques of recording. It follows a rigid procedure. It is a systematic way of questioning process with the respondents. The questions will be framed in advance and explanation will be procured from the concerned persons.

Unstructured interviews provide much freedom to ask the questions to the respondents. It is useful to the researcher, because it does not require any systematic procedure. It is casual conversation process. It gives an ample opportunity to researcher to conduct the interview as per his convenience. It is a flexible approach of questioning method. It do not follow any rigid laws and procedures. It does not require any standardised technique of recording information. In this method the researcher can omit or add same questions while conducting interview process. He may even change the sequence of questions. This method has some certain limitations The analysis of the responses becomes much more difficult and time consuming process. It requires more knowledge and abilities of the interviewer, otherwise it may be wasteful exercise. It is useful in case of exploratory or formulative research studies. Structured interviews are useful in case of **descriptive studies**. It is more economical and provides lesser skill on the part of interviewer.

Interview is a reflection of many factors hidden at the hearts of respondents. The behaviour of respondents will be measured by the interviewer. The researcher will appoint interviewers for carrying out this specialised task. Conducting of an interview and recording their responses are not an easy task. It requires specialised skill and abilities. Interviews further can be classified as:

(a) Focussed Interview
(b) Clinical Interview
(c) Non-directive Interview

***(a)* Focussed interview** means, starting a conversation with the respondent by the interviewer. It concentrates to get information from the respondents, which is based on the basis of their experience. It is mainly to share the experience of the respondents. The interviewer has freedom to design and prepare the sequences of questions. He can ask questions as per his convenience. It is a conversation based assignment.

***(b)* Clinical interview** is related to procure the information regarding individuals life experiences. It is concerned with recording of feelings and opinions of the individuals. Individual's life experience feelings will be known by the interviewer. The interview process will be completed as per the interviewer's choices.

***(c)* Non-directive interview** is associated with getting the information on a given topic to the respondent. In this method, the interviewer is simply encourage the respondent to talk on a specified topic. He will act as a catalyst to express the respondent's feelings and beliefs.

Interview is one of the best sources of collection of information to achieve the research object. Personal interview method has several advantages and disadvantages. The following are the advantages regarding this method.

Advantages

(a) Interview method provides more information to the researcher.
(b) It can generate more in-depth analysis of information to the researcher.
(c) It provides greater flexibility to the researcher to ask the questions as per his choices.

(d) It provides spontaneous personal information to the researcher.
(e) The language level can be selected as per the standards of educational qualification of the respondents.

Disadvantages

(a) Interview method of collection of information is a very expensive method.
(b) This method is not possible to access all respondents at any time.
(c) It is useful for only large and widely geographical samples.
(d) It provides scope for bias on the part of the interviewer.
(e) It creates headache of supervision and control of interviewers.
(f) High networth individuals, top level management executives, important higher rank officials, technocrats and bureaucrats may not be accessible to get interview for collection of information from them.
(g) It requires more time consuming process.
(h) Sometimes respondents may provide imaginary information for make the interview interesting.
(i) It requires a lot of training procedures for the field staff.

Hence, the personal interview method has several advantages and disadvantages. However, the researcher should be careful, attention and cautious approach while conducting interview method. He should be honest, sincere, hardworking and impartial. He must have a wide knowledge about the process. He should be a technical competent and have practical rich experience in this field. The researcher should make occasional field visits to monitor the activities of the interviewers. He should see, no interviewer may not deviate the process of interview method. The interviewers also should have behaviour with courteous and most respectable manner. The researcher should observe all his interviewers must behave with respondents as friendly nature conversational and unbiased. The interviewer should record original answer or feelings of the respondents. He should not show any partiality.

(B) Telephonic Interviews: Telephone interview is another method of sources of collecting information from the respondents. In this method, the interviewer can contact his respondents on telephone for getting the information. It is useful in industrial surveys. It is not widely popular in India. But developed nations follow this procedure. After development of the telecommunications sector in India, there will be more opportunities for using this device to contact the respondents in this way. It is more flexible way of operation than any other. It is faster than other methods. It is more economical and cost per response is very low. Frequent contacts with respondents is more easy and accessible. The process does not require any field staff. The interview may be conducted with the respondent at any time, any distance, any location. With the development of **cellular services**, it is easy to conduct this method of collection of interview through **Short Message Services (SMS)** and **Multimedia Message Services (MMS)**. SMS is a more popular way of method of collection of sources of information. But its not popular in India. An interviews can also be conducted through **"E-mails"**. The researcher can also use the internet services to complete his interview process. Sophisticated technology may reduce the cost of operations of the interview. Let us hope that, in future, the researcher may use **Short Message Services (SMS)** as a device for smooth functioning of his research work. Mobile phases are the best providers to get the information from the respondents at any time. This method has several disadvantages also. The respondents should own a phase otherwise it may not possible to conduct interview. In this method, the interviewer has little time to ask questions as phase. He has to complete the process quickly. Sometimes, there will be disturbance in the conversation between interviewer and respondents. The respondent may provide vague and reckless answers. Hence this method has not become popular in India.

(c) Questionnaire Method

The information may also be collected from questionnaire method. It is quite popular in India. It is more useful in case of large research projects. There will be a chance to take large number of samples for the study. This method is adopted by government organisations, research institutes, private companies and research scholars. It is ideally suitable for qualitative research programmes. It is more useful in economic and business surveys. In this method, a list of questions will be prepared by the researcher related to his research areas and sent to the various respondents by post. The respondents are requested to answer the questions and return the questionnaire. A questionnaire consists of a number of questions typed in sequence for a clear understanding by the informants. The questionnaire method can be further categorised as **structured** and **non-structured study**. Structured study means, the questionnaire contains a number of questions with a prescribed sequence. The researcher will prepare the questions in order to enable the respondent to fill the questionnaire without ambiguity. **Non-structured study** means, the questionnaire do not contains no sequence. Hence there is no prescribed sequence of questions exists in the study. The questionnaire method can also be further divided into two methods. They are **(a) Disguise, (b) Non-disguise study**. Disguised study means the objective of questionnaire is not clear. The informants does not know the questionnaire needs information. If the questionnaire has been with a clear objective, it is known as non-disguised study.

The questionnaire method has several advantages and disadvantages. However, the success of this method depends upon the abilities of the researcher. The researcher should draft the questionnaire in a proper way for thorough understanding of the contents. The questionnaire must be prepared with a simple language and expressions of meaning and concept. The success of questionnaire method depends upon the cooperation of the informants. All informants are able to answer the questions. If the questionnaire is in a readable form. The questionnaire must provide prepaid postage facility to the respondents. This method also have several disadvantages. The response is uncertain from respondents. Some respondents may reluctant to answer the questionnaire.

Merits

(1) Questionnaire method provides low cost expenses.
(2) It is useful for large and widely geographical samples.
(3) There is no bias of the interviewer.
(4) The respondent answer the questions in his own feelings.
(5) It provides sufficient time to the respondents.
(6) Respondents are freely reachable through post.
(7) This method is more useful to elicit more information from the respondents.

Limitations

(1) It is only possible, when the respondents are educated and behaves in a cooperated manner.
(2) It involves uncertainty in getting replies from the respondents.
(3) The explanation or answers of the respondents may not be accurate.

The collection of information is more important technique in getting the adequate and accurate data. The questionnaire is a tool to get sufficient information from the respondents. Questionnaire refers to a device for securing answers to questions by using a form which the respondent fills in himself. A good design of questionnaire reduce many problems and provides sufficient analysis. Drafting a questionnaire is a highly specialised job. It requires a great deal of skill and experience. The questionnaire requires some general principles while drafting. The following general principles should be followed for a better questionnaire form.

(A) Covering letter
(B) Size of questionnaire
(C) Sequence
(D) Simple language
(E) Clarity
(F) No scope for personal information
(G) Instructions
(H) Simplified questions
(I) Pre-testing the questionnaire

(A) Covering letter: The researcher should write a covering letter to the respondent enclosing the questionnaire. In the covering letter, he must convey the message about the research work. He should prepare the covering letter by introducing himself and indicating about the survey's objects. The covering letter should be a simple. The letter should indicate the importance of the survey. The researcher should enclose a prepaid postage cover for getting reply from the respondents. The researcher should inform the respondent that after getting the reply, the informants will not be disturbed again. Hence, there should not be a frequent questioning process.

(B) Size of questionnaire: The researcher should be more careful in designing the questionnaire. The size of questionnaire should be in minimum. The number of questions should be minimised. The researcher should ask only necessary information. The number of questions should be kept to the minimum. An ideal number of questions should be **15 to 20**. Unnecessary questions should not be incorporated in the questionnaire. It should be remembered that the number of questions will determine the response of the informants.

(C) Sequence: The researcher should keep in mind that the questions must be asked in a sequence. If there is no sequence of questioning, the respondent will get confusion in answering the replies. Hence, the researcher should avoid the confusion from the minds of respondents. The questionnaire should be built with spontaneous and natural way of sequence to enable to understand by the informant. The sequence of questions should be constructed carefully in term of the purpose of the research.

(D) Simple Language: The researcher should use a simple language of communication. He must keep in mind about the educational standards of the informants. The served questions should be short and simple. They must be asked in a simple language to enable all levels of educated people. A high standard of language is necessary for higher educated informants. The researcher should avoid ambiguous questions. He should not create any wrong notion of information.

(E) Clarity: Clarity is the most important factor to get good result of responses. The accuracy of responses will depend upon the degree of clarity of the questions being questioned. First of all, the informant should be able to understand asked questions with clarity. Any dilemma or ambiguity in questions should be avoided. Hence the researcher should provide good clarity of enquiry to get the clear analysis from the informants.

(F) No scope for personal information: The researcher should try to avoid the personal information of the respondents. He should not ask the questions about income-tax, sales-tax paid by him. They may not be willing to provide answers in written forms. Any important information should be collected by the researcher through a personal interview. Even in interviews, the researcher should ask these delicate questions at the end of interview. Asking personal information questions will greatly influence the informants.

(G) Instructions: A good questionnaire may provide necessary basic instructions to the respondents. A brief introduction about the research theme should be provided for easy understanding of the research area. The researcher should clearly sate the last date for submission of the answers. He should also indicate the address clearly for reply to be sent by the informants. He should also send the instructions about units of measurements. He should design questions about the fact, not about the opinions.

(H) Simplified Questions: The researcher should keep in mind about the level of standards of questions being asked. He should prepare the questions as per the research objectives of the study. Questions requiring calculations should be avoided. As far as possible the questions should be of such a nature that they can be answered easily in **Yes** or **No**. This is an excellent technique to get the information very fastly. Sometimes, answer cannot be given in a single or two words. Questions may designed to get specific information from the informants. However, it is better to prepare thoughtfully selected questions to get the good results from the informants.

(I) Pre-testing the Questionnaire: After designing of the questionnaire, the researcher should conduct pre-test process before mailing it to the informants. Pre-testing is also known as **"pilot survey"**. Pilot survey can be conducted preliminarily as experimental basis. If the research project requires a large sample, it is necessary to conduct pilot survey. Pilot survey occupies an important position, when research project stipulates large account of samples. There are several advantages of pilot survey such as the researcher can find out the mistakes of the questionnaire. He will take care about all the things about the research projects.

(d) Schedule Method

Schedule is another method of collection of sources of information. Research means a collection of information regarding a specified area of specialisation for providing a solution to the problems faced by the community. Schedule is a document like a questionnaire, which will be filled in by the enumerators. Enumerators are specially appointed for this purpose to fill the respondents given answer. It is just like a questionnaire. The enumerators will reach the respondents and asking the questions contained in schedules, at the same time, their answers will be recorded in the proforma. In some situations, schedules will be handed over to respondents. If the respondent required help from the enumerator, he will help in filling the schedule.

Therefore, the enumerators will occupy a key role in this method. The enumerators should be well trained to handle these specific tasks. It is very useful in extensive enquiries. It can lead to fairly reliable results. It is quite expensive. It will be carried out by central government agencies or large organisations. The researcher should take care about selection of enumerators. Enumerators should be qualified, have abilities and capacity to work with accordingly.

(e) Miscellaneous Methods

In the digital world times, there are so many other methods used by big business organisations. They are presented below:

(1) Warranty Cards
(2) Projective Techniques
(3) Content Analysis
(4) Distributors Opinion
(5) Pantry Audits
(6) Consumer Panels
(7) Mechanical Devices
(8) Depth Interviews

(1) Warranty Cards is one of the sources of collection of information. Warranty cards are placed inside the package of a product. Consumer is requested to fill the card and sent back to the dealer. Cards are generally appear in a postal sized card and used by dealers of consumer durables to collect the valuable information from the respected consumers. The information required content will be printed as the card and it will be collected from the dealers by the business concerns. The big organisations will get the feedback information from the dealer through this sources of information. The company will get the first hand information about their consumers.

(2) Projective Techniques methods are introduced by psychologists for collection of information from the respondents. This method is also known as **Indirect Interviewing Technique**. This method is useful to know the pulse of the consumers. Researchers can know the underlying motives, intentions, feelings, expressions from the respondents. It plays an important role in attitude surveys or in motivational researchers. It requires intensive specialised training. The individuals response will not be recorded at their face value. The reactions of the respondents can be recorded in different ways:

(a) Word power
(b) Sentence completion tests
(c) Story test
(d) Attitudes test
(e) Puzzles
(f) Sociometry
(g) Pictorial technique
(h) Verbal tests

(a) Word Power: This method is one of the techniques to collect the information from the informants. In this method, the respondents are asked to check word power. This method is used to extract information regarding words which have maximum association. In this method, the respondent is required to mention the first word that comes to his mind, immediately, interviewer will read out each word from a list. **For ex:** If the interviewer says black, the respondent may say **red**. There will be combination of 50 to 100 words in this technique. The matching words will be mentioned by the informants. This method is more useful in marketing research to know the quality of branded product. All qualities of a product may be provided to the informants. The respondents may be asked to write brand names. This method is quick and easy to use. It yields reliable results. It is more useful in advertising field. We cannot ignore the importance of this technique in this advertising field.

(b) Sentence Completion Tests: It is an extension of word power test. In this method, the informants are asked to complete a sentence related to the product characteristics. Many kind of sentence will be placed before the respondent on the same subject. The researcher will gather all the informants responses and make analysis about the product characteristics. The exploration of sample members views enable the researcher to know about the product satisfaction.

(c) Story Test: Story test method requires the informant to write a story. The informants are provided enough of material to focus attention on the given subject. The informant is asked to complete a story.

(d) Attitudes Test: In this method the feelings or attitudes of the informants are observed. In this technique, the researcher may observe many characteristics of the informants. The attitudes of younger's will be know through dolls. The youngers are provided with the dolls and their feelings will be captured while playing with it. Dolls are joyful things to the kids, which are allowed to play with them freely. This test is also known as **Dolls Play Test**. It is more useful in sociology. The characteristics of the informants can also be known through their choice of colour, form, words, etc.

(e) Puzzles: In this method, the information will be extracted regarding specific ability of candidates. The information will be collected through indirect method. The informants are tested in different ways by providing long and short questions. This method is useful for testing the memory of all informants. Quiz, puzzles are becoming more popular way to technique to test the memory power of informants.

(f) Sociometry: Sociometry is a method related to study about the individuals relationship in a society. Society is a combination of different caste and religious people. It closely observe about the relationship among individuals in the society. It is an indirect way to observe the social relations. It reveal the attractions or repulsions between individuals. Generally these methods are conducted by the news agencies regarding **"popular personalities"** on the global basis. It is possible to study the underlying motives of the individuals. In this method, an attempt is made to trace the flow of information amongst groups. The new ideas are explored. In this method we can identify leaders and followers. It involves charts and pictures.

(g) Pictorial Technique: Pictorial techniques are related to ask the informants in pictures. There are several techniques presented below:

(i) Thematic apperception test
(ii) Rosenzweig test
(iii) Tomkins-Horn picture
(iv) Holtzman Inkblot test
(v) Rorschach test

Thematic apperception test is associated with study of pictures. The pictures are related to day to day events of the layman's life. It consists of a set of pictures. The respondents will be provided with pictures and asked to describe about the pictures. The investigator will draw conclusions after obtaining picture description from the informants. The informants analysis is the basis for characterisation of their nature and attitudes.

Rosenzweig test is related to cartoons. The test uses a cartoon format. The respondents are asked to write their opinion in an empty balloon space provided for the purpose in picture. The informants description reveal his characteristics. The researcher can assume the attitudes, beliefs, feelings, inner motives of the informants.

Tomkins-Horn picture test is related to study about the groups attitudes. It consists of **25** plates, each plate contains three sketches. These sketches may be arranged in different ways to portray a sequence of events. The responses are analysed by the researcher which reveal respondents attitudes and beliefs.

Holtzman Inkblot test is associated to observe the attitude and feeling of the informants. This test consists of **45 Inkblot** cards. These cards are based on colour, shade and other movements. Every response is obtained from the subject. The responses of a subject are interpreted at three levels of form appropriateness. The researcher can analyse the informants attitudes, beliefs and feelings. This method has several advantages.

Rorschach test is related to study about psychological factors of the respondents. It consists of 10 cards. These cards having print of inkblots. The respondents' responses will be analysed by the researcher. This method is frequently used by the researchers but the validity of test remains suspectable.

(h) Verbal Tests: Verbal test is related to observe the other person's habits. In this method respondents are asked to comment about other people do? **For ex:** Why do people consume **"Gutka or pan masala"**. The respondents will give their responses for people's behaviour.

(3) Content analysis: Content analysis is related to contents of documentary materials. Books, magazines, journals, newspaper, tabloids contents will be analysed. It is a quantitative analysis. It is related to qualitative analysis. This method examines about the value of content published books, magazines or newspapers. It is a simple level of analysis of the content. It involves review of research articles, books, journals, that have been published. It measures pervasiveness. It is an index of the intensity of the force. It is the study of the nature of the verbal material.

(4) Contributors opinion: Generally all manufactured goods are distributed by distributors or wholesalers. The distributors will collect the market information through salesman at regular intervals. The distributors will ask the salesman to provide information about market size, market share, seasonal purchasing pattern etc. The salesman provide first hand information about the consumer behaviour. It offers the most efficient way of evaluating the effect of sales. Sales trends can be predicted by the feedback information by the distributors opinion. The manufacturers will also involve in conducting the survey measuring the consumer behaviour. In this method, the consumers feelings will be measured through observation and not on data basis. This method is also known as **"store audits"**. Store audits are best way of evaluating the effect on sale of variations of different forms of promotion.

(5) Pantry audits: Pantry audit is related to study about the consumer's behaviour. It is a best technique to estimate consumption of the basket of goods by consumers. It involves in study of consumer attitudes very closely. The researcher collects information regarding quality of product, price, quantity, availability, etc. The data will be collected through records of consumer's pantry. It is closely associated to study about the types of consumers, types of brands, and their consumption patterns. Pantry audits are conducted through questioning process to get the information about consumption levels and purchasing habits. This method is often considered to yield accurate preference of the consumers. Hence the researcher will get actual needs of the consumers.

(6) Consumer panels: Consumer panel is an extension of pantry audits. It will be conducted on regular basis. The consumers are requested to maintain a detailed daily records of their consumption levels. A set of consumers who are grouped as a consumer panel, will be contacted by the investigator on regular basis. They will be interviewed repeatedly over a period of time. The consumer panels are of two types: **(a) Transitory consumer panel, (b) Continuing consumer panel. A transitory consumer panel** is a method to closely monitor the specified phenomenon. In this method a panel is conducted as a before and after basis. The researcher will conduct an initial interview before the phenomenon arises to record the attitudes of the consumers. The researcher will conduct another interview, after using the commodities or goods to record their feelings. It is more useful in advertising sector. **A continuing consumer panel** is set up for an indefinite period. The researcher will gather data in a particular aspect of consumer behaviour at a regular intervals of period of time. This panel is to find out in the area of consumer expenditure, public opinion and advertising sectors. These panels are operated through mail system.

(7) Mechanical devices: Mechanical device is another indirect method way of collection of information. The information will be collected from the informants through mechanical devices. Technology provided more sophisticated devices to extract the information from the informants. The researcher can use latest electronic equipments such as **Audiometer, motion picture camera, eye camera, pupilometric camera, psychogalvanometer, etc**. All these electronic gadgets are used by the researchers for big organisations. **Audiometers** are used by television channels to record the audience favourite programmes watched by them. It is a device to measure the viewers preference in watching the television programmes. It records the changes in viewing programmes by the audiences. **Motion picture cameras** are used to record the transaction while the buyer making purchases at shops. It will be used to shoot the consumer while they are purchasing from the big stores or from a shop. The consumers are attracted by beautiful packages. The consumer's hidden movements can be recorded through inside of the supermarkets. All these information is more useful in analysing the market estimation or predictions. Prediction is the most important factor for making business decisions. **Eye cameras** are the best devices to measure the feelings of the respondents. They are designed to measure the eyes of respondents on a specific portion of a sketch. It is more useful in advertising sector. **Pupilometeric** camera is used to record a visual stimulus. **Psychogalvanometer** is a device which records the body excitement as the result of visual stimulus. All these sophisticated technological devices are useful in capturing the feelings of the informants.

(8) Depth Interviews: Depth interviews are designed to explore the inner feelings of the informants. It is one of the kind of interview. It is planned to explore needs, desires and feelings of the respondents. It helps to observe the psycho-social relations of the respondents. These interviews should be planned with greater skills. The interviewer should have higher capabilities to tackle the situation. This kind of interviews require more time and cannot be executed within a short period of time. The researcher should have more knowledge, abilities and skills. It is an emotional interview. The respondents sometimes go for emotional situations while they reveal their past life. They will reveal past experience, past life, their hardships, hurdles faced by them can also be explored. The respondents ambitions, desires, can be exposed to the public. Famous personalities, popular leaders, cine heroes, artists, celebrities, dynamic persons attitudes and beliefs can be captured. These interviews are more useful to the researchers to incorporate their feelings, emotions, sharing rich experience, providing message to the society. The popular personalities life history is the inspirational sources for the upcoming or dynamic personalities. However, some persons can reluctant to give answers asked by the researcher.

(b) Secondary data

Data consists numerical information. Numerical numbers express more information. Secondary data means, the data is already available. The data someone collected and utilised by others. The secondary data can be used by a number of researchers. It can be used by anyone, for any purpose. Hence the secondary data are compiled by someone other than the user. Data which is not originally collected but rather obtained from published or unpublished sources are known as secondary data. **For ex:** Census data will be used by several researchers. The secondary data occupies a dominant role in the statistical work carried out by many investigations. A data which is primary in the hand of one become secondary in the hands of another. Secondary data is a cheapest source of information. It does not require any expenses like hiring enumerators, editing, tabulating, printing, etc. Researcher alone can utilise the information for his research purpose. Secondary data can be procured faster than primary data. Researcher must be careful in using data. Secondary data may be unsuitable or may be inadequate in all ways. Secondary data should have some characteristics for reliability. The secondary data must possess the following characteristics:

(a) Reliability
(b) Accuracy
(c) Adoptability

(a) Reliability of the data is most important factor in determining the quality of investigation. Research project constitutes a number of statistical analysis. Statistical analysis contains with full of data. Secondary data reliability can be judged out by the person, who collected the information. The reliability of the data depends upon the sources of information, proper using methods, nature of bias of compiler etc. The researcher before using the secondary data, he should think about all these factors.

(b) Accuracy of data is another important factor for incorporating the data in the research project. The researcher should take care about the accuracy of the data. The findings of the research result depends upon the accuracy of the input. If the level of accuracy of the data is found inadequate and it should not be used by the researcher.

(c) Adaptability of the data may not be possible in all ways. The data, which is prepared for one enquiry purpose, does not found suitable for another enquiry. Hence the researcher should be careful in modifying or converting or adopting data for his own research purpose. Research studies are different from one another. Unsuitable data should not be used by the researcher at any time. In this situation, the researcher should take all precautions in adopting the data for his research purpose.

Researcher should be used data only when he finds them reliable, suitable and adequate. He should not discard the data unnecessarily. An intelligent researcher with due precautions can utilise the information according to his needs and convenient. The method of collection of secondary data constitute the following factor:

(1) Research objectives
(2) Funding agency
(3) Period

(1) Research objectives is the most important factor in selection of appropriate method for data collection. It requires collection of information regarding research area of specialisation. It depends on observation of information. The enquiry method depends upon the objective of the project. The researcher should think about the method of data collection either through **primary** or **secondary data**. He should choose the collection of data as per the suitability of his study.

(2) Funding agency is one of the important factor for the smooth functioning of the project. Available of funds may helpful for easy completion of the study. The data collection, compiling, editing, tabulation, computations, analysis, appointment of project staff, contingency staff, field expenses, all these activities will be carried out by the researcher with the availability of the funds. An adequate flow of funds helpful to complete the project as per schedules. If the limited fund is available, the researcher will have to select a cheaper method to complete the study. Hence it may not be efficient and effective as some other method costly. **Fund** is a big constraint in India for carrying out research work either in social science or in **life sciences.**

(3) Period of the project requires the researcher to complete his study in a planned time. The researcher should make his plans as per the collection of data. The collection of data requires a lot of time for searching information. Information is the most powerful device at the hands of the researcher. It may be utilised by the researcher as per his study. Generally all UGC projects requires to complete in **2 years. Major research project** may require to complete in 3 years. Research projects at Indian Council of Social Science Research requires to complete the projects from **3 months to 24 months.**

Research in India depends upon availability of funds. India has sufficient manpower and excellent skilled scientific technical pool of resources available at low cost. At present, sophisticated mechanical devices, tools, latest software make the researcher for easy completion of the study. Collection of data is the main important task in the research project. Each method of data collection has its own use and none is superior in all situations. **For ex:** Telephonic interview method may be adopted for easier and fast collection of data. It may be used for few degree of questions related to research objects. In case of collection of more information, **personal interview** method is relatively better. If the time is sufficient, funds are scarce than mail questionnaire can be treated as best method. In case of a wide geographic area is to be covered, the use of questionnaire is more better than other methods. **Personal interview** will yield more reliable information and more information may be procured. Hence the most desirable approach with regard to the selection of the method depends on the nature of the particular problem and on the time and resources available along with the desired degree of accuracy. Therefore, the researcher should prepare his own plans as per his research study.

Case study

Case study method is related to **qualitative analysis**. It is more popular method to study a unit, or a person or a family. It involves a careful and complete analysis a specified object. It completely observe a unit and make analysis. The community can also be observed in this method. It is an in-depth analysis for a particular aspect of the study. It involves complete analysis and study a limited events or conditions. It is an intensive investigation of a particular group under observation. The main object of the case study is observe the behavioural patterns of a given unit. It is just like post-mortem of the living person. It is a fairly exhaustive study of a person or an organisation. It is also known as **"social microscope"**. It is related to study the organisation up to in minute details. The inferences will be drawn on extensive and in-depth analysis of the organisation. The study covers all facets of the organisations that are operative in nature. It is not a quantitative analysis approach. It gives a clear insight into life. It also provides better solutions, problems faced by the organisations. It also observe mutual interrelationship of casual elements. It is a direct study and not indirect method of enquiry. In this method hypothesis can be tested and enables the generalised knowledge will get more richer and richer. It is a widely used systematic research based scientific technique used in social sciences. It was introduced by **Frederic Le play** in his studies of research. **Herbert Spencer** introduced to use case material in his comparative study of different cultures. Now-a-days all social scientists utilised this method in their research methods. Management experts uses this method more frequently. It provides clues to several management problems. It is based on several assumptions. They are:

(a) It is a psychological aspect of analysis but human behaviour may vary according to situations.
(b) It is related to study of the natural history of the organisation.

Case study method requires the following steps to make a research study on a specified organisation.

Step I Identification of the problem of an organisation

Step II	Collection of data, verification of history
Step III	Diagnosis test, remedial treatment
Step IV	Application of treatment tests
Step V	Follow up programmes

The case study method has several advantages and disadvantages. They are presented below.

Advantages

Case study method is an observation of behavioural pattern of the social unit. A researcher can analyse the organisational history and may suggest measures for improvement of the unit. This method provides more knowledge to the researcher regarding the environment of universe. In this method, the researcher can use any method to collect the information such as **depth interviews, questionnaire, interviews, study reports etc.** It provides intensive study of a social unit. Hence, it is repeatedly used by all researchers in their study. It also provides to study the nature along with a social unit. It is related to historical analysis of a social unit. The researcher get feelings of personal experience regarding study of a social unit through the case method. It provides a perfect type of sociological material regarding a social unit. It helps to take managerial decisions in solving several problems of the unit. It provides a latest study method to record a minute study of the different facets of the organisation. The researcher can understand the social change. It also helps in drawing of inferences and valuable suggestions may be provided. A well thoughtful, research based techniques will definitely yield better returns to the organisations.

Disadvantages

Case study method has several disadvantages in study of a social unit. Information procured by the researcher through this method is often not comparable. It provides information its own way. The actual information may not be collected in this process. It provides false generalisation of information. It is not possible to study the problem through sampling method. It is not suitable for large units or big society.

Research Engine

Global consultancies[1] and local firms are setting up research units in India to take on work for companies around the world. In 1998, global consulting major **McKinsey & Co.** set up a pilot centre to service the research needs of its offices in London and Sydney. Today, the McKinsey Knowledge Centre, as it is called, houses **300 odd** employees and supports McKinsey's worldwide offices with three separate teams. Global consulting bigwigs like **Bain and Co., Frost and Suvillan** and the Everest group have followed McKinsey with captive research units in the country. Apart from these, third party providers like **Genpact, Evalue Serve, WNS, Office Tiger, Copal Partners, Pipal Research** and a host of others also offer research services to clients. These companies work with consulting firms, equity research companies, investment bank and the like to provide information that supports core functions including strategic planning business development and sales planning. **Office Tiger**, a professional services firm, has about 120 people, who will work in research functions. Overall it is estimated that about 2000 to 3000 professionals are currently employed in the field of business research. **WNS Knowledge** services has a 100 people strong business research team. The business research opportunities being offered by firm in India will be different from other countries. Knowledge processing outsourcing firms offer employees international exposure to economies, firms and business scenarios that will widen their world view. **Market Research** is another area that has grown with the emergence of the KPO model in India. **WNS** estimated that about 11.5 per cent about 1400 of the 12,000 people employed in KPO were in the MR (Market Research) area. Market research deals with survey design, followed by primary data collection, analysis, insight generation and presentation. **For ex:** a company may outsource a project to understand the chocolate consumption habits of children in the **4-14** age group. A marketing research firm that takes on outsourced work would their devise the survey, questionnaire, collect data through telephonic or web based interviews, analyse the data using software tools like quantum, synthesis the data and elicit relevant insights and finally, present the finished product to the client. Data collection can be done by undergraduates, or graduates, while graphic design skills are needed for the presentation part. Higher and skills come into play for survey design, data and statistical analysis and the task of using judgement to derive insights. For these, firms usually hire people with maths, science, statistics or computer science background. MBAs, Engineers or anyone with a quantitative bend of mind could find employment here. Survey design and insight generation would require people with an understanding of the market research field as the complexity involved is greater. Companies like Evalue Serve, WNS, Ineva, Office Tiger, Pipal Research, Ugans, Exenova India and Annik Systems offer services in the MR space. In addition to these domestic MR, like Market Research Bureau and AC Nielson also conduct outsourced work of this nature for their clients. For those already in the market research field, switch from a domestic company to a KPO is not very hard compensation levels are higher by **30-70 per cent** and career growth is quicker as the MR outsourcing industry is expanding. **KPO** offers benefits in terms of financial rewards and career progression, professionals should be willing to work larger and more erratic hours.

NOTE

1. The Research engine, *Economic Times*, Monday 14-11-05, p. 7.

5

ANALYSIS OF DATA

Data occupies an important tool in research study. It consists of a numerical information regarding a specified object. It expresses the trend an situation of the environment. After collection of data, the researcher's task is to process the crude data into a finished product. The available data may not be directly utilised in research study. The data must be purified, processed and analysed as per the requirement of the study. Scientific study requires a relevant data for making comparisons and analysis. The available data generally lie in crude method. It should be processed such as editing, coding, classification and tabulated in a systematic way. Analysis of data constitutes computation of various measures to compare in a systematic way of study. Authorities in this subject reveal that processing and analysis is the same. Both functions convey same meaning and reflections. They conclude that analysis of data means a number of closely related operations which are collected and synchronised in a scientific manner to answer the research questions. The statistical tools will be used for inferring the research problem. The collected data may not be easily understandable. The analysis required two important functions such as **(a) classification, (b) tabulation**. Classification and tabulation provide a clear picture of information to the researcher.

Classification

After collection of data, the next step is to purify the data. Further processing of collected data is called as **"classification"**. Classification is making groups of related facts into one class. All numerical information will be grouped on the basis of similar characteristics. Facts are collected by investigators and similar characteristic numericals will be classified. All research studies collect a large volume of raw data, which may be reduced into homogenous groups. The process of arranging data in a specified group or a class is known as classification. The data will be grouped on the basis of similar characteristics. **For ex:** sorting of letters at post offices. Letters are grouped on the basis of their destinations. Letters with destination **Mumbai** will be placed in a particular bag. **Chennai** will be put in a specified bag as per their destinations. They are put in a separate bags and transmitted through various modes of transport. **For ex:** Generally students will apply to get admission into a college through application forms. The application forms will contain all particulars regarding their personal and academic affairs. Their applications will be processed and a merit list will be prepared on the basis of their previous examinations performance. Classification has several objectives. Classification may minimise the laborious work of the researcher. We can show the millions of figures in a systematic and simplified manner. Classification of data will facilitate easy comparison. The classification of data enables the researcher to avoid unnecessary elements in the data. Generally the data can be classified on the following basis:

(A) Geographical classification
(B) Chronological classification
(C) Qualitative classification
(D) Quantitative classification

(A) Geographical classification

Data contain numerical informations. Data can be classified on the basis of areawise. It is known as geographical classification. In this method data will be grouped on the basis of states, cities, regions, zones and mandals. **For ex:** Production of wheat in India can be expressed as follows:

Production of Wheat 2004-05 Statewise (Actuals)

	Name of the State	*Production (million tonnes)*
1.	Andhra Pradesh	30
2.	Assam	40
3.	Bihar	45
4.	Haryana	82
5.	Uttar Pradesh	85
6.	Madhya Pradesh	65

The geographical classification can be arranged in the order of alphabetical order or on areas ranking method.

(B) Chronological Classification

Chronological classification means, data will be categorised on the basis of a period of time. The data may be presented on yearwise basis. The figures of population of a nation production particulars of a company, sales details of a company. **For ex:** Population of India from 1951, 1961, 1971, 1981, 1991, 2001 etc.

(C) Qualitative Classification

Qualitative classification enables to classify the data on the basis of its nature or quality. The data can be categorised on the basis of sex, colour of hair, literacy, religion, casts, etc. **For ex:** the classification of population can be divided as **Urban or rural, literate or illiterate, male or female, employment or unemployment,** etc.

(D) Quantitative Classification

Data will be classified on the basis of quantity. The data regarding height, weight, income, sales, profits, production can be classified in this method. In this method a frequency distribution may be prepared in order to get a meaningful way of presentation. Frequency distribution can be prepared in discrete and continuous classes. Hence it requires an elaborative classification process.

Tabulation

Tabulation is the simplest method of expression for summarising data. A table is a systematic way of presentation of data in several columns and rows. Table will provide a meaningful comparison of various elements. After classification of data, the next step is involved in tabulation. Tabulation will make data easier to understand by the reader. The researcher can present a huge mass of data in a simple manner of presentation. It occupies an important place in the research study. Tabulation will avoid unnecessary material and repetition of data. It provides for easier way of comparison. It can be done by manual or by mechanical or electronic devices. In large enquiries of samples, mechanical gadgets will be applied for tabulation process. Manual tabulation is enough for small enquiries. It can also be categorised as **"simple"** and **"complex"** tabulation. Simple tabulation is related to one or more groups of independent questions. **Complex** tabulation categorises the data into two or more categories. Information will be provided one or more set of inter-related questions. Simple tabulation is related to one-way tables. Complex tabulation is related to two-way tables, three-way tables or higher order tables. These tables are known as cross tabulation. Tabulation should be done as per the needs and requirements of the researcher.

Principles of Tabulation

Statistical tables can be constructed on the principles of tabulation. Tabulation reveal the division of data in two or more categories. Tables supply information about several interrelated characteristics of the data. The following principles are related to a good table:

(a) All tables must be specified title with a clear and concise and placed above the body of table.
(b) All tables must be assigned distinct number for easy reference.
(c) Tables should be made as logical, clear, accurate and simple.
(d) Tables should be arranged in chronological or alphabetical or geographical to facilitate meaningful comparison.
(e) Tables should have indicated sources of information.
(f) Abbreviations should be avoided.
(g) All figures should be rounded off to avoid unnecessary details in the table.
(h) Tables should not use **"Ditto"** marks.
(i) Tables should use in percentage and ratios.
(j) Tables should not be overloaded with more details.

Data Processing

Data indicates representation of all numerical information processing implies the following steps:

(a) Editing
(b) Coding

(a) Editing is a process of purification of raw data. The collected raw data should be prepared in a scientific way. It is useful to detect errors and omissions for a better understanding of the information. It involves a careful observation of the crude data. It makes data more accurate and consistent. Editing may be categorised as **Field editing** and **central editing.** Field editing will be done by the interviewer after completion. It will be completed on the very day or on the next day. The investigator should not correct errors of omission by simply guessing. **Central editing** is related to take place after completion of interview. All forms or schedules should be completed and return to the office. A single editor is enough for small study of research work. A team of editors are required for large sample size of the study. All forms may be edited thoroughly by the editors. Any review work in research study should be carried out by the editors. Editors are well trained and scientific educated persons, who thoroughly verified the collected data. Sometimes, correspondents will contact the interviewer for any clarification. Editors must be careful at performing their work. He must give familiar instructions to the interviewers. He must put signature and date of reference on the forms or schedules.

(b) Coding is another process of purification of the raw data. It refers to process of assigning numericals. All collected data must be arranged in a systematic way for easy reference. Sometimes the collected data may be assigned with symbols. All responses will be categorised into a limited number of classes. It is necessary for efficient analysis. The researcher should think about coding while designing questionnaire. Coding may be done either manual or through computer system. Manual code method requires some standards and regulations. The researcher should think about the reducing of errors in coding process. However, the researcher should be more careful in processing of the data. He must be more cautious in completion of tabulation and coding process.

Problems in Processing

Processing is a method of synchronisation of information. There is no difference between processing and analysis. Analysis is the summarisation of collected raw material. Processing stage is the most important factor in the research study. Generally researchers face problems while processing data. They are:

(a) Unclear response
(b) Numerical information

(a) Unclear response or don't know responses are difficult to handle. Generally statements are assigned with appropriate alternative answers. One category of such responses may be **"don't know"**. If these responses are small, there is no significance change on the results. If it is relative big, it will become a matter of major concern. A good researcher should always try to avoid the complicated responses.

(b) Numerical information may be used in the form of percentages. Percentages are used in data presentations. Percentages indicate the simplification of numerical work. It makes us to facilitate the data for a meaningful comparison. The researcher should not use large percentages. A large percentage is difficult to understand the content. Percentage may hide the real data. The reader may not be understandable actual situation.

Analysis

Analysis means a detailed examination of the study. It involves in computation of certain indices. It refers to estimation of unknown parameters of the population. It may be useful in testing of hypothesis and making inferences. Analysis can be categorised in two ways:

(a) Descriptive analysis
(b) Inferential analysis

(a) Descriptive Analysis: Descriptive analysis is related to study the large sample of distribution of single variables. It provides to study about the profile of business organisations, persons and work groups. It is also known as **"undimensional analysis"**. Analysis regarding one variable in-depthly is described as descriptive analysis. Analysis regarding two variables can be termed as **"bi-variate analysis"**. Analysis regarding more than two variables can be described as **"multi-variate analysis"**. Hence, it should be remembered that various measures show the size and shape of a distribution. Nowadays analysis function of research work were made easy with the help of introduction of information technology. Computers are more useful in research studies. They simplified the process of research work and enables for easy compilation. Analysis can be further classified as **Correlation** and **Casual analysis. Correlation** analysis is the study of relationship between two variables. It refers to the study of joint variation of two or more variables. **Casual analysis** is the study of observation of one or more variables which affects each other. It is also referred as **"functional relationship"**. It is also known as **regression analysis**. Casual analysis is useful in carrying out experimental research. **Correlation analysis** is useful in social and business research studies. After introduction of information technology methods analysis has been made more convenient to the researchers. A tremendous development has been occurred in **Multi-variate analysis**. All statistical methods will be applied to analyse more than two variables on a sample of observations. **Multi-variate analysis** can be categorised **"Multiple regression, multiple discriminant analysis, multi-variant analysis of variance, canonical analysis"**. Multiple regression analysis will be applied for study of two or more independent variables. It is useful to make predictions about the dependent variables. **Multiple discriminant analysis** is related to study about a single dependent variable. It can be categorised two or more groups on the basis of similar attributes. It is based on to predict an entity's possibility of belonging to a particular group. **Multivariate analysis** is an extension of two-way classification. It is also termed as analysis of variance **(ANOVA)**. It is a statistical technique specially designed to test the means of more than two quantitative populations are equal. It is capable of fruitful application to diversity of practical problems. It consists of classifying and cross classifying statistical results. **Canonical analysis** is related to study about predicting a set of dependent variables.

(b) Inferential Analysis: Inferential analysis is related to the tests of significance for testing hypothesis. Data will be tested and validity can be checked with scientific methods of the study. It is based on drawing of inferences. It is related to interpretational skills. It provides some conclusions or findings.

Statistical Tools in Research

Research means, exploring new things from universe. Universe consists of a number of hidden facts. All facts are not known by a man. Man is a human being with a limited role before nature. Man is a kid before universe. All hidden facts in universe are explored by the researcher by their intellectual thinking power. All facts are tested with the help of statistical tools. Statistical tools provide us a clear information about the facts collected by the researcher. Statistics in research has been occupying a dominant role in scientific study of investigations. Statistical tools are useful in analysing the data and making conclusions. Statistical tools can be used in large sample of populations and useful in reducing the laborious work. It can be read easily and used for further analysis. Statistics cannot be ignored by either a social or life science scientists. Any researcher worker can be used by statistical tools in his study. Utilisation of statistics can be useful to the value addition of content. It stimulates the higher levels of standards of study. **Statistics** can be classified as **descriptive** and **inferential statistics**. Descriptive statistics is related to study of indices. **Inferential** statistics is concerned with the study of generalisation. It is also known as **"sampling statistics"**. It faces some problems like estimation of population parameters and statistical hypothesis. Generally research work contains some statistical measures. They are presented for a thorough understanding of the various parameters.

1. Averages
2. Dispersion
3. Skewness
4. Correlation
5. Miscellaneous.

1. Averages

Averages are one of the powerful statistical tools to analyse the data. It is a simplification of quantitative data. It describes the characteristics of the entire mass of unwidely scattered data. The word average is popularly known in a day to day operations of the layman's life. It is a single value that represents a group of values. Its value lies in between largest and smallest items. It is also known as **"measures of central tendency"**. It can also be termed as **"statistical average"**. An average is frequently called as **"measures of central tendency"**. It may represent the mass of data in one single value. It enables the researcher for better comparison of variables. Comparison can be made either at a point of time or over a period of time. The averages are useful in comparison of two or more groups of data. It should be remembered that the comparison should be done with some average tool for two groups. The good average should have some characteristics. The average should be easy to understand by the layman. Statistical methods should be designed to simplify complexity. An average should be simple to **calculate**. It is widely used by all possible people for their research work. It should not be involved in more complicated calculations. It should depend upon each and every item of the series. It should have a single means of way of expression of the data. It should be useful in further statistical computations. It should be capable of further use in algebraic calculations. The average should be capable of sampling stability. The following are the important types of averages. Mean, median and mode are the most popular averages.

(a) Arithmetic Mean
(b) Median
(c) Mode
(d) Geometric Mean
(e) Harmonic Mean

(a) Arithmetic Mean

Arithmetic mean is also called as **"Mean"**. It is most popular and widely used method. It represents the entire data in a single digit. Statisticians always use it or called as **mean**. Arithmetic mean value can be arrived by dividing the total of the values of various given items in a series by the total number of items. It is better than other averages. It is more useful in economies and business studies. Arithmetic mean can be classified as **"simple arithmetic mean"** and **"weighted arithmetic mean"**. Simple arithmetic mean can be calculated in all series, such as individual, discrete and continuous series. It can be computed in direct and shortcut methods. In this all theoretical aspects of the statistical tools have been presented for acquiring more theoretical knowledge. Research methodology is a subject for beyond the level of post-graduation. Hence readers are requested for calculations, please refer "statistical" books for thorough understanding the subject. Arithmetic mean is widely used in practice. It has several advantages and disadvantages. It is a simple average method for easy understanding the subject. It is effected by the value of all items in the series. It is relatively reliable data. It provides the centre of gravity. It is based on calculation value but not as a positional value. It has several **limitations**. It is greatly impact by extreme values. It cannot be completed without making assumptions in a distribution with open-end classes. It is always not useful as a good measure of central tendency. It provides a characteristic value and may not likely to serve a useful purpose. **Weighted arithmetic mean** gives equal importance to all the items. It is useful in problems relating to construction of index numbers and standardisation death and birth rates.

(b) Median

Median is called as positional average. It refers to the place of a value in a series. It refers to the middle value in a distribution. It can be computed by arranging the data in ascending or descending order. It is widely used in qualitative research studies. It is not widely used in sampling statistics. It has several advantages. It is more useful in case of open-end classes. It can also be computed in unequal classes. It may not be influenced by extreme values. It can be presented graphically. It has also several limitations. It requires arranging the data either in ascending or descending order. Its value is not determined by all items in the distribution of sample items. It is not capable of algebraic treatment. It is affected by more through sampling fluctuations. It can be computed exactly as in the case of mean.

(c) Mode

Mode is one of the tool in averages. Mode is a positional average. It is not affected by values of extreme one. It is useful in all situations. It is the most repeatedly occurring value in a series. In a distribution, where a digit repeatedly occurs, is called as **Mode**. It is the size of the item which occurs repeatedly. It is useful in the study of popular sizes. It is also called the most typical or fashionable value of a distribution. It reveals about most common income, most common height, most common size of shoe, factors to enable the understanding of the context with clarity of meaning. It is easiest way for computation. Mode can be calculated in all series such as in individual series, discrete series and continuous series. Sometimes two values will occur with equal frequency in the distribution of sample. Then it is called as **bi-modal**. In a bio-modal distribution, mode cannot be determined through graph method. Hence mode can be determined through the following formula:

Mode = 3 Median – 2 Mean

Mode has several advantages and disadvantages. It can be used as to describe qualitative phenomenon. It is useful in finding consumer's preferences. It has also some limitations. The value of mode cannot always be determined. It is not capable of algebraic manipulations. Mode is known as a symmetrical distribution.

(d) Geometric Mean

Geometric mean is specially useful in certain areas. It is theoretically considered as best average for construction of index numbers. It is frequently used in determination of average per cent of change. It is based on each and every item of the series. It is rigidly defined. Geometric mean is defined as the **nth root** of the product of the values of "n" items in a given data.

(e) Harmonic Mean

Harmonic mean is based on the reciprocals of number averaged. Its value is based on every item of the series. It is related to computation of velocity of an article. It is useful in comparison of variables with constant quantity of another variable. It is not easily understood. It is not useful in analysis of economic data. It has also several limitations. It has little practice application and is not good measurement.

All of the averages have their own limitations and advantages. However, the researcher has to make selection for some statistical averages. There are no hard rules and rigidity for the selection of a particular average. The selection of an average mostly depend on the nature, type and objectives of the research study.

2. Dispersion

All averages are useful for presentation of data in a simplified manner. It reduces the laborious research work. But averages cannot expose the entire story of any research study. The averages cannot disclose the scattered values of items in distribution of variables. In this situation, the scattered data will be measured by another tool is known as **Dispersion**. It helps us in studying the important characteristics of a distribution. It is the measure of the variation of the items. It provides an average of the differences of various items from an average. It is also known as **variation**. It gives an average of the difference of various items from an average. The variation reveals the amount of degree but not the way of direction. It is helpful in determination of the reliability of an average. It is useful in comparison of two or more series of the samples. If the sample is very large, the average may not be quite reliable. In this situation, variation is more useful to the researcher. It is more useful in social science for studying special problems such an inequality of the distribution of income or wealth. Measures of variation can be used in powerful analytical tools in statistics such as correlation, testing of hypothesis, analysis of variance, regression analysis and statistical quality control. A good measure of dispersion should be simple and easy to understand. It should not be required to problematic computation. Computation process must be simple. It should be based on each and every item of the distribution. It should be manageable for algebraic treatment. The following are the important methods of studying variations:

(a) Range
(b) Quartile deviation
(c) Mean deviation
(d) Standard deviation
(e) Lorenz curve

(a) Range is the simplest method of studying dispersion. The difference between smallest and largest value of the items given in the distribution. The smaller range indicates less dispersion and the average of that distribution is more typical of the group. It is useful in quality control department in the corporate sector. It is more useful in preparation of control charts. It is also useful in stock market operations. Stock market is a highly volatile market. It involves fluctuations in day to day operations. It is useful in comparison of share prices from one period to another. Commodity price range can also be completed. The weather situations of the nature can be determined with the help of range. The meteorological department utilises this tool for arriving maximum and minimum temperature on a particular day. This information is greatly helpful to the public. It is also most commonly used measure of dispersion in everyday life of the layman. It is more useful in business and economic aspects of the research studies.

(b) Quartile range or quartile deviation is another measure of dispersion. It has also certain limitations. It is based on two extreme items. It does not take into consideration of the numerical data scatter within the range. Quartile deviation is a superior method than range. It is useful in computation of open-end distribution of the sample. It can also be useful in measuring erratic or badly skewed distributions. It ignores half of the distribution of the sample. It cannot be manageable in mathematical implications.

(c) Mean deviation is also called as average deviation. It will be computed through deviations taken from average. It can be computed through averages such as mean, median and mode. It is simple to understand and easy to compute. It is useful for general public. It is based on each and every item of the data. It is less affected by the value of the extreme items. It has also several limitations. It ignores algebraic signs in computation process. It may not yield accurate result. It is not capable of further algebraic treatment. It is not popularly used in sociological studies. It is more useful in study of **"Forecasting business cycles"**.

(d) Standard deviation is extremely useful in presentation of a represented data in a simple way. It is widely used measure of studying dispersion. It is free from some defects. It is also known as **"Root square deviation"**. It measures the absolute dispersion. A small standard deviation means a high degree of uniformity of the observation. It can be computed in all series of the data. It can be computed through actual, assumed and step deviation method. It is widely used tool in all research studies. It can be manageable for mathematical implications. It is most prominently used in further statistical work.

(e) Lorenz curve is one of the graphic methods of studying dispersion. It is useful to measure the distribution of wealth and income. Researchers can use this curve in the study of degree of inequality in the distribution of profits, wages and turnover. It is useful to study the cumulative percentage in all economic and financial aspects of the corporate sector.

All the above measures can be used according to the situation. These tools can be used as per the available data. Standard deviation may be avoided where the sample contains extreme values. Quartile deviation can be used in open-end classes. Mean deviation can be avoided in case of generally skewed data. Generally average deviation would be acceptable. Standard deviation is the most popular method in study of measurement of variability. It is amendable to mathematical manipulation. It is less affected by fluctuation of sampling. It is most widely used device in the context of estimation and testing hypothesis.

3. Skewness

Skewness is a device to measure asymmetrical of the sample. If the distribution of all items in a series happens to be perfectly, it is known as symmetrical. Skewness can be further classified as positive and negative. In case of positive skewness, the order of average in such a manner

$\mathbf{Z < M < \bar{X}}$. The order of the negative skewness is like $\mathbf{< \bar{X} < M < Z}$.

4. Correlation

Study of Relationship

All numerical information contains data. Data represents the facts. The facts are tested by statistical tools. The statistical tools study the behaviour of data. The study of one variable in the population is known as **univariate population**. If the study is related to measure two variables in the population will be called as **"bivariate population"**. The study of two or more variables is known as **"Multi-variate population"**. Every measurement of a variable A, we have corresponding value of a second variable B. The resulting pairs of values are termed as a bivariate population. Multivariate population is related to study of A, B, C, D and fifth variable. In these measures we wish to know the two or more variables in the data is known as "relationship analysis". There are two kinds of measures to study the population:

(A) Bi-variate population
(B) Multi-variate population

(A) Bi-variate population: A study of two variables related to measure the variables are known as **Bi-variate population**. The study of relation between variables are known as **correlation**. Correlation can be studied through

1. Cross tabulation

2. Spearman's rank correlation
3. Karl Pearson Coefficient of Correlation

Cross Tabulation is useful for measuring the relation between variable in the sample of data. In this method, each variable can be divided into two or more categories. The each category is subdivided again in order to get the relationship as symmetrical, reciprocal or asymmetrical. **Symmetrical** relationship reveals, which the two variables vary together. **A reciprocal relationship** expose the relationship when the two variables mutually influences each other. **A symmetrical relationship** reveals that one variable is responsible for another variable.

Spearman's rank correlation is another technique to determine the degree of correlation between in the context of ordinary data. The relation will be observed by assigning ranks to the samples of the study. It is a non-parametric technique for measuring relationship between variables.

Karl Pearson's correlation is also called as simple correlation. It is most widely used method for studying the relationship between two variables. The degree of relationship between the variables under consideration is measured through the correlation analysis. It is useful in understanding of the economic behaviour. In corporate sector, it is useful to estimate costs, sales, prices and other variables. It can be classified as follows:

(a) Positive or negative correlation
(b) Simple, partial and multiple correlation
(c) Linear and non-linear

Positive correlation means a change in the direction of two variables in the same way. Both variables show either increasing trend or decreasing. **Negative correlation** means, one variable is increasing the other is decreasing. Both variables are moving towards opposite direction.

Simple correlation means study of relationship between two variables. In this method only two variables relation will be observed. **Partial correlation** is related to study about relationship between three or more variables. **Multiple correlation** to study the relationship between three or more variables simultaneously.

Linear correlation means a change in ratio on fixed basis. The ratio of change between the two variables is the same. **Non-linear**

correlation is a change in one variable which does not bear a constant ratio to the other variable.

(B) Multi-variate population: Multi-variate population is related to study the measurement of two or more variables. It can be studied through the following measures:

1. Co-efficient of multiple correlation
2. Co-efficient of partial correlation
3. Multiple regression equation

Regression is a statistical tool to measure the relationship between two or more variables. One variable influences another variable. It is a statistical method to deal with the formulation of mathematical model. It depicts the relationship amongst variables which can be used for the purpose of prediction of the value of dependent variable.

Attributes

Attributes is the method to measure the degree of relationship between two aspects. The data will be classified on the basis of a particular attribute. The objects may possess any more attributes. The association may be positive or negative. The association of attributes can be studied through the following methods:

(i) Expected frequencies method
(ii) Proportion method
(iii) Yule's coefficient of association
(iv) Coefficient colligation
(v) Coefficient of contingency

Expected frequencies method is applied to study the actual observation with the expected data. If the actual observation is equal to the expectation, then there will be independent attribute. If the actual observation is more than the expectation, the attributes are said to be positively associated and if the actual observation is less than the expectation, the attributes are said to be negatively associated. It provides information not only on the nature but also on the degree of association.

Proportion method is related to study the nature of association and not the degree of association.

Yule's coefficient of association is the most popular method of studying association of attributes. In this method, not only we can determine the nature of association but also the degree or extent to two attributes are associated. It is useful to compare the intensity of association between two attributes.

Coefficient of colligation is developed by Yule. It is denoted by the symbol **Y**. Coefficients are not directly comparable with each other.

Coefficient of contingency is a frequency table in which a sample from the population is classified according to two or more attributes.

5. Miscellaneous

The measure of studying association of attributes can be made through the following processes:

(a) Index numbers
(b) Analysis of time series

Index numbers are useful in measuring the relative changes. A change in economic and social phenomena can be measured and compared through index numbers. Index numbers are barometer of the economy. The index number is a specialised average to measure the change in a group of related variables over a period of time. A change in single variable is known as **univariate index**. An index which is constructed from a group of variables is known as **composite index**. Index numbers measure the effect of changes over a period of time. They are most widely used tool for measuring over a period of time. They also compare economic conditions of different locations. They are indispensable tools of economic and business analysis. Business policies are guided by index numbers. Employees salaries are paid by the level of index numbers. The living standards of the citizens and inflation levels will be determined by the index numbers. They are most widely used in many fields of the society. Sociologists refer the index numbers to measure the population indices. Psychologist use index numbers to measure intelligent quotients of persons. Health authorities, educational institutions utilised the index number to measure the effectiveness of the sectors. Index numbers also reveal trends and tendencies. It is useful in studying the effect of seasonality and cyclical for us. They are highly useful in studying the general business conditions. They are also useful in forecasting future economic activities. They may classified on the basis of:

(a) Price
(b) Quantity
(c) Value
(d) Miscellaneous.

The index numbers can be constructed on the basis of **Unweighted Indices** and **Weighted Indices**. These indices have several limitations. They are based on samples. They can also be misused in such a manner to draw the desired conclusions. They are constructed on different methods yield different results. The indices are constructed from samples deliberately selected samples. Therefore analysis of data can be shown as follows for a better understanding about the indices.

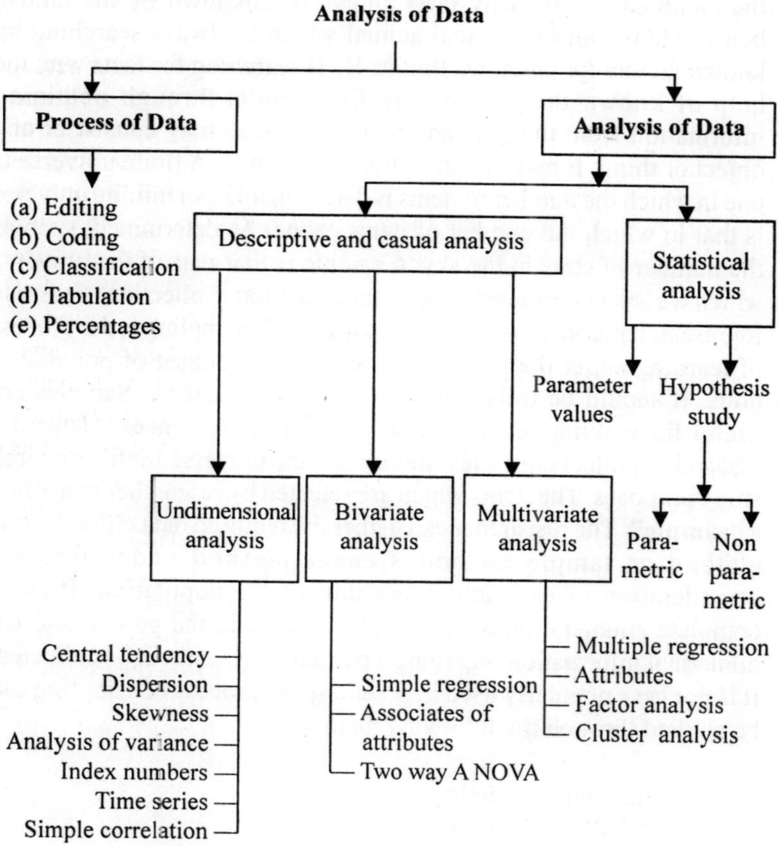

6

FUNDAMENTALS OF SAMPLING

Research means exploring new things from the universe. Universe is the combination of many facts known or unknown by the human being. Man is an intellectual animal which is always searching by known factors for unknown things. He is searching for facts with the help of known things. He may find results through obtaining information from the population. The universe may consist of any object or thing. It may be either finite or infinite. A finite universe is one in which the number of items is determinable. An infinite universe is that in which the number of items cannot be determined, such as the number of stars in the sky. A sample is that part of the universe which we select for the purpose of investigation. Collection of sample for research purpose is known as **"sampling"**. Sampling is the process of learning about the population. Sample is a subset of population units. It should be truly representative of population. Samples are useful for making generalisation or to draw inferences. Generally researchers select only a few items from the universe for his research study purposes. The items which are selected by researcher constitute a **"sample"**. The researcher can gather the required data either census method or sample method. **Census method** undertakes for consideration of each and every unit of the population. It takes complete enumeration of all things available in the population. All numerical information regarding a particular aspect will be collected. It is not very popularly used in practice. The process of sampling can be studied through the following methods:

(a) Selection of sample
(b) Collection of information
(c) Drawing inferences

Generally all research projects are carried out by the social scientists. They prepare research themes for completion of study. The smooth completion of the research project can be executed by the researcher in a proper way. Selection of sample is the most important factor to meet the research objectives of the study. As per the objectives of the study, the researcher can make his selection regarding various items to be collected. After identification of the sample, the researcher will go for further next process is known as **"collection of data"**. Collection of data is another important function of the researcher. He will make designs for easy collection of information. **For ex:** A doctor examines a few drops of blood and draws inferences. The researcher will make inferences on the basis of collected sample. Hence sampling is a tool to find the conclusions regarding a research problem. A sample study is less expensive than a census study. It provides accurate measurements. Sample study requires a well-trained and experienced investigators. The following concepts and principles can reveal complete meaning of the **"sampling method"**.

(a) Universe
(b) Sampling process
(c) Significance levels

(a) Universe

Universe refers to the total of the items or units in any field of research investigation. It undertakes all aspects and all units of the elements into consideration. All units in any field of inquiry constitute universe. Population and universe of the two terms are the same and interchangeable. Population means the total of items about the information is desired population constitute similar characteristics of all the elementary units. Elementary units possess similar attributes of the object of study. The aggregate of elementary units is generally described as population. The universe can be finite or infinite. If the population contains a fixed number of elements, then it is said to be **"finite"**. **For ex:** the population of a town. In finite, the number of items will be known by the researcher. The number of items will be known as **"N"**. The symbol "N" is usually reveal the number of items associated in the study. An **infinite** population means, it is impossible to observe all the elements. It has unlimited elements. It cannot be enumerated in a specific period of time. We cannot have any idea about the total number of items. **For ex:** number of stars in the sky.

(b) Sampling process

Sampling Process is another method for carrying out the research study. The elementary units are the main basis for sampling process. A list containing all sampling units is known as sampling frame. The research project has to complete within a time horizon. Researcher can use telephone directory for conducting opinion survey in a city. Sample process will be executed through a sample design. Sample design is a plan for procuring data within the horizons. It can be determined before any data collection. All statistical tools will be applied for measuring the characteristics of the population. The description of characteristics of the population is known as **"parameter"**. Parameter is a limit defining the scope of an activity. It is a statistic which constitutes the objective of sampling analysis. Generally surveys constitute the study of a small portion of the sample. In conducting surveys, there may be possible to occur errors in the sample. Hence it is known as **"sampling errors"**. Sampling errors are also termed as **"error variance"**. Sampling errors generally arise while gathering samples from the population. These errors are inversely related to the size of sample.

(c) Significance level

Significance level is related to the reliability of the expected results. **For ex:** If we take a confidence level of 95% means, there will be 95 chances of true data from 100. Confidence level indicates the likelihood that the answer will fall outside that range. We always remember that if the confidence level is 95%, then the significance level is 5%. If the confidence level is 99%, the significance level is 1%. The significance level indicates the answer within the purview of range. The specified confidence level constitute the either acceptance or rejection regions. Sampling analysis is based on sample distribution. Sample is useful to compute various statistical measures like **mean, standard deviation**. Every sample may yield its own value for the statistics under consideration. A large sample may expose closer to the normal distribution. Hence a mean of sampling distribution will be on par with the mean of universe. Sampling distributions can be used for:

(a) Mean
(b) Proportion
(c) Students distribution (T-test)
(d) "F" distribution
(e) Chi-square distribution

Sampling distribution of mean may tend quite closer to the normal distribution. A large sample may be called when the sample items exceeds 30. It is very useful in several decision situations for accepting or rejection of hypothesis. It refers to the probability distribution of all the possible means of random samples of a given size from the population.

Proportion is an important tool in sampling distribution. It is useful to find out defective parts in a large number of samples. It reveals about the success of a thing for testing hypothesis. N indicates sample size of the data.

Students "T" distribution was formulated by **W.S. Gosset (1876-1937)**. He was an employee of **Guinness & Son,** Ireland. The firm did not permit employees to publish research findings under their names. Hence he adopted the **pen** name **"student"** and published his findings through this name. It becomes more popular as **"T-test"** in academic community. It ranges from minus infinity to plus infinity. It is symmetrical and has a mean zero. It is more useful for computation for small size sample. Small size sample constitute less than 30 items of data. It is generally used to test the significance of the various results obtained from small samples. They are presented below to test the significance of:

(a) Mean
(b) Between means of two samples (independent sample)
(c) Between means of two samples (dependent sample)
(d) Correlation co-efficient

After computation process ends, the results should be compared with the **"t" table**. The calculated value of **"t"** is less than the table value, the hypothesis is accepted. If the calculated value of **"t"**, is more than the table value, the hypothesis is rejected.

"F" test is also known as the **"variance ratio test"**. It is named in honour of the "RA Fisher". The object of the test is to find out whether the two independent estimates of population variance differ significantly. It is based on the ratio of two variances. It is based on the assumptions such as **Normality, homogeneity and independence of error**. The calculated value of **"F"** is less than the table value, the null hypothesis is accepted. The calculated value of "F" is greater than the table value, then the null hypothesis is rejected.

Chi-square test is most widely used non-parametric test in statistical work. It is originated from sociological and psychological research work. It is very popular in behavioural sciences. It is most widely used in business research. It is the simplest form of a statistical work. It was first used by **Karl Pearson**. It describes the magnitude of the discrepancy between theory and observation. It is very popularly known as test of goodness of fit for analysis. The calculated value of chi-square is compared with the table value for given degrees of freedom at a certain specified level of significance. The calculated value is more than the table value of chi-square, the difference between theory and observation is considered to be significant. The calculated value of chi-square is less than the table value, the difference between theory and observation is not considered as **"significant"**. Probably, sometimes it may be misused.

Sampling Theory

Sampling theory is related to random samples. Sample is the part of universe. It is selected for the purpose of investigation. It studies the relationships that exist between the universe and the selected samples. It is concerned with estimating the properties of the population. The movement of sample towards universe is known as **"statistical inferences"**. A universe is the complete group of items in a related area of knowledge. Sampling theory is designed to attain the following objectives:

(a) Estimation
(b) Testing of hypothesis
(c) Statistical inferences

Statistical estimation means knowing the population parameters from known sources of information. It helps us to know unknown things from the facts. It is based on sample statistical estimation can be done for a point estimate or an interval estimate. The point estimate is a single estimate in the form of a single form. **Interval estimate**

are used in statistical induction. It has two limits, i.e., upper limit and lower limit. It may lie between these two points.

Testing of hypothesis is another objective of the sampling theory. A hypothesis is a supposition made as a basis for reasoning. It is simply a quantitative statement about a population. Sampling theory enable us to decide whether to accept or reject hypothesis. It helps in determining whether observed differences are actually due to chance or they are really significant.

Statistical inference is a branch of statistics. It occupies a dominant role to deal with uncertainty things happening in the nature. It is related with using probability concept. It refers to the process of selecting and using a sample from population to draw conclusions. It treats two different classes of problems, i.e., hypothesis testing and estimation. Sampling theory helps in making generalisation about the population. It is based on samples drawn from population. It provides accurate generalisations.

Sampling theory is associated with the study of relationships between a population and samples. It is related to random samples only. A universe is a combination of different facts. Sampling theory can be studied under two heads:

(A) Sampling of attributes
(B) Sampling of variables

Sampling of attributes is related to study of the qualitative characteristics of the items in a population. A sample which consists less than 30 items is known a **"small sample"**. A sample which consists more than 30 items of the population is called as **"large sample"**. Statistics of attributes can be studied in the form of two kinds, i.e., **one method** consisting of items in the attribute is present. Another method of class of consisting of items where attribute is **absent**. The presence of attribute appears is called as **"success"** and its absence is known as **failure**. The sampling distribution generally takes the form of binomial probability distribution. The binomial distribution tends to become normal distribution. It is used for sampling analysis. Sampling of attributes faces three kinds of problems such as parameter value comparing with observed data. Sometimes the parameter value is not known by the researcher and it has to be found by estimation it from the sample. Another problem is reliability of the estimated value. All these problems may be overcome through using the appropriate standard errors.

Sampling of variables is another study of sampling theory. In this method, the theory can be applied for comparison between observed and expected values of the fluctuations arises from samples. It can also be applied for estimation of population parameters from the sample. The sampling theory can be used to find out the degree of reliability of the estimation. The test of significance used for both large and small samples. Large samples contains normal sampling distribution and close to the population values. **Small samples** are not covered by the sampling theory. Small samples contains less number of items and cannot assume the sampling distribution is approximately normal. For this purpose a new technique adopted for handling small samples is known as **"T" test**. "T" test is based on "t" distribution and through it made significant contribution to small samples. It will be used for samples less than 30 items and the population variance is not known. It can be used for testing the values of the samples and then compare with the table value the calculated value of "t" is either equal to or exceeds the table value, we infer that the difference is **significant**. The calculated value of "t" is les than the table value of "t", it is not significant. We can test the significance of the **mean, correlation, partial correlation, correlated pairs, etc**. "t" test has been developed and simplified for computation of the difference between observed and expected value of the samples. An alternative approach has been developed to test the data. **Joseph Sandler** has developed an alternative approach, known as **"A" test**. It serves the purpose as is accomplished by "t" test relating to paired data. It is more useful to psychologists. It can be compared with table value. The calculated value is of "A" is equal to or less than the table value, it is considered as significant. The calculated value of "A" is more than its table value, it is considered as **"Insignificant"**. The values of "t" and "A" are inversely related. "A" test is relatively simple. It saves time and labour.

Standard Error

Standard error is an important factor in sampling theory. Standard deviation of sampling distribution is termed as "Standard error". Standard error helps us in the following dimensions:

(a) Chance
(b) Reliability
(c) Horizon

(a) Chance Error: The standard error reveals the difference between observed and expected frequencies that arises due to chance. The difference between observed and expected values is less than **3 times**. The standard error, the difference exists due to chance factor only. If the difference is equal to or more than **"3" times** the difference existed not by chance factor. Hence the difference is a significant difference.

(b) Reliability: Reliability is the most important factor in statistics. The data reliability occupies a dominant role in determining the decisions. The standard error has smaller value there is greater uniformity in the sampling distribution. If the standard error value has higher content, then the reliability of data is doubtful. The unreliability of the sample is more. Therefore, the reliability depends upon the size of the standard error.

(c) Horizon: Standard error helps us to specify the limits within the horizon of parameters of the population. It specifies the degree of confidence. It indicates interval. This interval is known as confidence interval.

Standard errors can be measured through the following situations:

(a) S.E. in case of sampling of attributes
(b) S.E. in case of sampling of variables (large samples)
(c) S.E. in case of sampling of variables (small samples)

Estimation

Estimation is the most important factor in statistical analysis. Statistical research studies does not know population parameters. The population parameters are not known by researchers. They estimate the population parameters may be a single value or a range of values. A good estimator has to possess same characteristics. An estimator should be unbiasedness. An estimator should have a relatively small variance. An estimator should have much information. The researcher must select appropriate estimators for his study. The researcher can estimate the following widely used concepts:

(A) Estimating population mean
(B) Estimating population proportion

(A) Estimating population mean: A large sample approximates the normal distribution. The sample mean is the best estimator of the population mean. If a researcher knows the sampling distribution of mean, he may estimate from the sampling information. Every sample mean is a separate point estimate of the population mean. A researcher can estimate that will hold for a much smaller range he must either accept a smaller degree of confidence in the results. Otherwise he can take a sample large enough to provide this smaller interval with adequate confidence levels. Hence the sample size increases, it yields the desired interval estimate and the degree of confidence.

(B) Estimating population proportion: Sample proportion of the units is best estimator of the population proportion. Large sample may approximates the normal distribution. If a researcher wants to construct confidence interval to estimate a population proportion, he should use the binomial distribution with the mean of the population. If the sample size increases, the financial distribution approaches normal distribution. It is useful for estimating a population proportion. Standard error of proportion can be defined as the mean of the sampling distribution of the proportion of success is taken as equal to the standard deviation for the proportion of success.

Sample size is also one of the influential factor in sampling theory. The size of the sample occupies an important factor in statistical analysis. If the sample size is too small, it may not serve to achieve the objectives. If the sample is too large, it may involve high cost and laborious work. Therefore, the researcher has to select an optimum size of sample. It should not be either large or too small. The sample size should be large enough to give a confidence interval levels. Size of the samples are influenced by the following factors:

(a) Universe
(b) Accuracy
(c) Miscellaneous Factors

Universe is a combination of different factors in nature. It may contain either homogenous or heterogeneous in nature. A small sample reflects the characteristics of homogenous in nature. The items of large samples contains heterogeneous characteristics in the universe. A large sample can provide groups and sub-groups of items. A small sample might not be able to provide a reasonable number of items in each group. The sample size is based on intensive study. The sample size should be small. A small size sample is quite suitable for continuous study. It provides full information about the nature of the characteristics of the items. **Large sample** of items provide better environment for conducting general surveys. A small sample is suitable for technical surveys.

Accuracy is another important factor in the sampling theory. A large sample provides a higher level of standard of accuracy. For enhancing the accuracy of the standard levels, the sample size should be increased substantially.

Miscellanceous factors also influences the size of sample. **Funding** of the project occupies an important factor in determining the size of the sample. The size of the sample depends upon the amount of money available for the study purposes. A large sample result in increasing the cost of estimation. **Time** is another important factor for completion of the research project. **Questionnaire, trained investigators** availability may provide for easy completion of the research project. The researcher should pay proper attention while selecting the sample size.

Hence the determination of the size of sample depends upon two alternatives. According to first approach, the precision of estimation influence the size of the sample. Second approach is based on **Bayesian** theory. It is theoretically optimal, but it involves difficulty in measuring the value of information. The **First approach** is capable of providing mathematical solutions. It is frequently used technique in determining the number of items in the sample to be covered. It does not analyse the cost of collection of data and expected value of information. Therefore, generally researchers depend upon the first approach.

Graded Illustrations

Illustration 1: From the following information construct a 95 per cent confidence interval for the mean age of managers in Mumbai.

From a random sample of 72 managers, it was found that the mean age 40 and standard deviation 4.5 years.

Solution: The confidence interval level can be computed as follows:

95% of confidence interval for the mean age of population

$$\overline{x} \pm z \frac{\sigma_s}{\sqrt{n}}$$

$\overline{x} = 40$ z = at 95% confidence level is 1.96 (as per the normal curve area table) $\sigma_s = 4.5$; $\sqrt{n} = \sqrt{72}$

$$\therefore \quad 40 \pm 1.96 \frac{4.5}{\sqrt{72}}$$

$$\text{or} \quad 40 \pm 1.96 \frac{4.5}{8.49}$$

$$\text{or} \quad 40 \pm 1.96\ (0.53)$$

$$\text{or} \quad 40 \pm 1.03 \text{ years.}$$

Illustration 2: In a random sample of 42 finance professionals, it was found that their mean age 35 and standard deviation 3.75 years. Calculate mean age of finance professionals at 95 per cent confidence interval levels.

Solution: The confidence interval level can be calculated as follows:

95% of confidence interval for the mean age of population

$n = 42$

$\bar{x} = 35$

$\sigma_s = 3.75$

$z = 95\%$ 1.96 (as per the normal curve area table)

$$\bar{x} \pm z \frac{\sigma_s}{\sqrt{n}}$$

$$35 \pm 1.96 \frac{(3.75)}{\sqrt{42}}$$

or

$$35 \pm 1.96 \frac{3.75}{6.35}$$

$$35 \pm 1.96\ (0.59)$$

$$35 \pm 1.15 \text{ Years}$$

Illustration 3 : From a random sample of 60 of the 2000 intersections in a city, the average number of two wheeler accidents per year was 3.85 and the sample standard deviation was 0.95. You are required to (a) estimate standard deviation of the population from the sample standard deviation, (b) calculate standard error of mean for this finite population, (c) at 90% confidence level, what will be upper and lower limits of interval level and calculate mean number of accidents per year?

Solution: Available information can be presented as follows:

$N = 2000$
$n = 60$
$\overline{x} = 3.85$
$\sigma_s = 0.95$
$z = 90\%$ confidence level is 1.645 (as per the normal curve area table)

(a) The best point estimate of the standard deviation of the population is the standard deviation of the sample itself.

$$\cdot\sigma_p = \sigma_s = 0.8$$

Standard error of the finite population is as follows:

$$\sigma_{\overline{x}} = \frac{\sigma_s}{\sqrt{n}} \times \sqrt{\frac{N-n}{N-1}}$$

$$= \frac{0.95}{\sqrt{60}} \times \sqrt{\frac{2000-60}{2000-1}}$$

$$= \frac{0.95}{7.75} \times \sqrt{\frac{1940}{1999}}$$

$$= \frac{0.95}{7.75} \times \sqrt{0.97}$$

$$= \frac{0.95}{7.75} \times 0.98 = 0.12$$

Calculation of upper and lower units at 90% confidence interval for the mean

$$x \pm z\left[\frac{\sigma_s}{\sqrt{n}} \times \sqrt{\frac{N-n}{N-1}}\right]$$

$= 3.85 \pm 1.645\ (0.98)$
$= 3.85 \pm 1.612$

Illustration 4: XYZ Iron Ore Company has estimated the average quantity of material to be 40 tonnes per shift and the sample standard deviation will be 3.2 tonnes per shift based upon a random selection of 4 shifts. Construct a 90% confidence interval around this estimate.

Solution: $\bar{x} = 40, \sigma_s = 3.2, n = 4, t = 90\%$ is 2.353 for 3dt (as per the table of "t" distribution)

Population mean can be computed as follows:

$$\bar{x} \pm \frac{\sigma_s}{\sqrt{n}}$$

$\bar{x}$ = 40

t = 90 % 2.353. (n – 1) = 4 – 1 = 3

σ_s = 3.2

$$40 \pm 2.353 \frac{3.2}{\sqrt{4}}$$

$$40 \pm 2.353 \frac{3.2}{2}$$

$$40 \pm 2.353\ (1.6)$$

$$40 \pm 3.76$$

Illustration 5: A consumer goods company conducts a market research survey regarding the study of impact of advertisement. For this purpose the marketing department contacted 70 consumers, they informed that 60% of consumers were motivated by the advertising. Calculate the confidence limits for the proportion of consumers motivated by the advertisement. It should be calculated at 95% level of confidence.

Solution: At 95% of confidence level, the standard variate is 1.96 (as per the normal curve area table)

$$P \pm Z\sqrt{\frac{P.Q.}{n}}$$

P = Proportion of consumers motivated by advertising in the population

Z = Standard variate (95% level is 1.96)

n = 70

P = 60% or 0.60

Q = 1 – P

$$Q = 1 - .60 = 0.40$$

$$= .80 \pm 1.96 \sqrt{\frac{(0.6)(0.40)}{70}}$$

$$= 0.6 + 1.96 \sqrt{0.003}$$

$$= 0.6 + 1.96\ (0.058)$$

$$= 0.6 + 0.11368$$

= lower limit 48.63%

= upper limit 71.36%

Illustration 6: Hindustan Lever Ltd. conducts a market survey. The company contacted 55 consumers to know about the impact of advertising. They informed that 65% of consumers were motivated by the advertising. Find out the confidence limits for the proportion of consumers motivated by advertising in the population. Calculate the proportion of consumers at 95% level of significance.

Solution: Calculation of proportion of the consumers at 95% level of significance

$$P \pm Z\sqrt{\frac{PQ}{N}}$$

N = 55, P = 65% or .65, Q = 1 – P = 1 – .65 = 0.35

Z = 95%, 1.96 (as per the normal curve area table)

$$0.65 \pm 1.96 \sqrt{\frac{(0.65)(0.35)}{55}}$$

$$0.65 \pm 1.96 \sqrt{\frac{0.2275}{55}}$$

$$0.65 \pm 1.96 \sqrt{0.0041}$$

$$0.65 \pm 1.96\ (0.06)$$

$$0.65 \pm 0.12$$

upper confidence limit 77%

lower confidence limit 53%

Illustration 7: A researcher taken a sample of cereal containers for the universe of 6000. The information is available for us for making analysis.

Total sample size is 4000 for the universe.

(a) The variance of weight 8 ounces on the basis of past records.
(b) You are required to estimate within 0.16 ounces of actual average weight with 99% probability.

What is the change in size of sample. If we assume infinite population in the given situation.

Solution: The confidence level at 99% can be calculated as follows:

$$x \pm z\frac{\sigma_p}{\sqrt{N}}\sqrt{\frac{N-n}{N-1}}$$

The sample size (n) can be found as

$$n = \frac{z^2 \cdot N \cdot \sigma_p^2}{(N-1)e^2 + z^2\sigma_p^2}$$

N = 4000
σ_p = 2.82 (since the variance of weight = 8 ounces)
e = 8 Ounces
z = 2.57 (at 99% level confidnece, as per the table of area under normal curve)

$$n = \frac{(2.57)^2(4000)(2.82)^2}{(4000-1)(.8)^2 + (2.57)^2(2.82)^2}$$

$$n = \frac{(6.6049)(4000)(7.9524)}{(3999)(0.64) + (6.6049)(7.95)}$$

$$= \frac{210099.22}{2559.36 + (52.52)}$$

$$= \frac{210099.22}{2611.88} = 80.43$$

Hence, he sample size is 81 for the given precision and confidence level in question with finite population. If the population taken as infinite, the sample size will be computed as follows:

$$n = \frac{z^2\sigma_p^2}{e^2} \qquad z = 2.57$$

$$\sigma = 2.82$$
$$e = 8$$
$$n = 4000$$

$$n = \frac{(2.57)^2 (2.82)^2}{(0.8)^2}$$
$$= \frac{(6.6049)(7.9524)}{(0.64)}$$
$$= \frac{52.5248}{0.64} = 82.07$$

Illustration 8: In a simple random sample selection, researcher drawn a sample from the population items of 4500. If the sample contains 3 per cent of the defective of the true value with 95.5% probability. What should be the size of sample? If the population is assumed to be infinite in the case.

Solution: The size of sample can be drawn in the following way:

N = 4500
e = 0.03 (estimation should be within 3% of true value)
Z = 2.005 (as per table) of area under normal
P = 0.03

Curve for the given confidence level of 95.5%

$$n = \frac{Z^2 PQn}{e^2 (N-1) + Z^2 PQ}$$
$$= \frac{(2.005)^2 (0.03)(1-0.03)4500}{(0.03)^2 (4500-1) + (2.005)^2 (0.03)(1-0.03)}$$
$$= \frac{(4.02 \times 0.03)(0.97)4500}{(0.0009)(4499) + (4.02)(0.03)(0.97)}$$
$$n = \frac{(0.1206)(4365)}{4.0491 + 0.116}$$
$$n = \frac{526.41}{4.1651} = 126.38$$

If the population happens to infinite, then the sample size will be as follows:

$$n = \frac{Z^2PQ}{e^2}$$

$$n = \frac{(2.005)^2\,(0.03)\,(1-0.03)}{(0.03)^2}$$

$$\because \frac{(4.02)\,(0.03)\,(0.97)}{0.0009}$$

$$= \frac{0.116}{0.0009} = 128.88$$

Illustration 9: The following information is related to a five star hotel. The management of the hotel is interested to know about the guests who stay for more than 4 days. The reservation manager wants to be 95% confident that the percentage has been estimated to be within ± 4% of the true value. What is the sample size required for taking a decision.

Solution: Population is infinite.

The size of sample can be computed as follows:

$$n = \frac{Z^2PQ}{e^2}$$

$Z^2 = 1.96^2$ (as per table of area under normal curve for the given confidence level of 95%).

P = 0.5

Q = 0.5

$$n = \frac{(1.96)^2(0.5)(0.5)}{(0.4)^2}$$

$$n = \frac{(3.8416)\,(0.5)\,(0.5)}{0.0016} = \frac{0.9604}{0.0016} = 600$$

The ideal size is 600 items.

Illustration 10: Taj hotel provides the information relating to guests movements. The management is interested to know the guests who stay for more than 2 days. The lobby manager wants

to be 95% confident that the percentage has been estimated to be within ±2% of the true value. You are required to find out the conservative sample size of the guests for making business decisions.

Solution: $n = \dfrac{Z^2PQ}{e^2}$

Z = 1.96 (as per table of area under normal curve for the given confidence level of 95%)

P = 0.5

Q = 0.5

e = 2 days

$$n = \frac{1.96^2(0.5)(1-0.5)}{(0.02)^2}$$

$$n = \frac{3.8416(0.5)(0.5)}{0.0004}$$

$$n = \frac{0.9604}{0.0004} = 2401$$

The most conservative sample is 2401.

7

TESTING OF HYPOTHESIS (Parametric and Non-Parametric)

Statistics contains statistical inference. Statistical inference has had fruitful development. It refers about population. Hypothesis is an important tool in research. It is the principal instrument in social science research. It is useful in conducting experiments and observations. Experiments are carried out by the researcher with an object of testing hypothesis. It enables us to make probability statements about population parameters. It provides a way to conduct new experiments and observations. Hypothesis test the validity of an experiment, which is based on the available information. Social science is a combination of different aspects of the thoughts. These thoughts may be proved scientifically with the help of various statistical techniques. **Hypothesis** means a mere assumption. It is to be proved or disproved with the help of statistical techniques. The researcher wants to test the available information, as a part of his investigation. Research hypothesis is a predictive statement. It is tested by various scientific methods. These tests are related from independent variable to some dependent variable. **For ex:** A coin may be tossed 300 times and we may get heads 120 times and tails 180 times. **For ex:** We may study the average weight of the 100 students of a particular college and may get the result as 125 kg. We may now be interested in testing the hypothesis that the sample has been drawn from a population with average weight 135 kg. **For ex:** Brand "A" four-wheeler is performing as well as brand "B". Hence hypothesis provides what we are looking for. It is a proposition to be tested for validity. Hypothesis provides valuable information to the researchers. The characteristics of the hypothesis is provided as follows:

1. Hypothesis should be clear and precise.
2. Hypothesis should be capable of being tested.
3. Hypothesis should be consistent with known facts.
4. Hypothesis should be in a simple manner.
5. Hypothesis should be in a position to explain the facts.
6. Hypothesis should be limited in scope and must be specific.

Procedure for Testing Hypothesis

Generally researchers want to test their experiments with a suitable, accurate device. The device is known as "hypothesis". The device should be used properly. For testing of hypothesis require the following procedure:

(a) Designing of a hypothesis
(b) Significance level
(c) Computations
(d) Decisions

(a) Designing of A Hypothesis

After taking a decision to test the available information, the researcher should set up a base for testing of hypothesis. The researcher should set up a hypothesis about a population parameter. He should collect the sample data as per the requirement of the study. He must assume a certain value for a population mean. He may compare the hypothesised value and the actual mean of the sample. Hence the difference is significant. The difference between these two values is smaller, the hypothesised value for the mean is correct. If the difference is larger, the hypothesised value for the mean is not correct. The traditional approach provides for construction of two hypothesis. If one hypothesis is accepted another will be rejected. In a statistical test, hypothesis can be categorised as follows:

(i) Null hypothesis
(ii) Alternative hypothesis

(i) Null hypothesis is a simple tool to test the significance. It is very useful to the researcher to test the difference in sample and population values. Null means "invalid", hence null hypothesis reflects no difference in the sample. The difference between sample and population values found in accidental and unimportant. It is based on a simple principle like "A man is innocent, until he is proved guilty". It is generally symbolised as $\mathbf{H_0}$ and alternative hypothesis is as $\mathbf{H_a}$. **For ex:** If we want to find out whether additional classroom teaching has benefited the students or not, we may set up a null that **"additional classroom teaching has not benefited the students". Another ex:** If we want to find out whether a particular brand is effective in curing leprosy. We will take the null hypothesis that, **"The medicine is not effective in curing disease"**. Hence the rejection indicates the differences which have statistical significance. The acceptance of the null hypothesis reveal that the differences are due to chance. Therefore, the rejection of the null hypothesis may reveal success in statistical report.

(ii) Alternative hypothesis is related to one, which everyone wishes to prove. The set of alternatives to the null hypothesis is referred to as the alternative hypothesis. If we accept null hypothesis then we are rejecting alternative hypothesis. If we accept alternative hypothesis, we are rejecting null hypothesis.

H_0 = Null hypothesis
H_a = Alternative hypothesis

(b) Significance Level

The second step is related to test the level of significance of a framed hypothesis. The difference between actual and population parameters can be listed through statistical devices. The significance level is described as percentage value. **For ex:** 5 per cent level of significance means, the researcher have a doubtful for wrong decision to the extent of 5%. **For ex:** 1 per cent level of significance indicates that there will be wrong choice of judgment to the extent of one per cent.

(c) Computations

The third step is associated with testing procedure of a hypothesis. It involves selecting an appropriate probability distribution for the particular test. T test, F test and chi-square tools are used to test the sample data. The sample size should be selected on the basis of circumstances.

(d) Decisions

The final step is to draw conclusions based on the statistical tools and devices. The statistical decision is a decision either accept or reject the null hypothesis. After making all computations, the result will be analysed by the researcher based on the test criteria. If we test the hypothesis at 5 per cent level and the observed set of results has probabilities less than 5 per cent, then the difference between the sample and observed parameters is significant. On the other hand if the difference is more than **5 per cent**, it is not significant statistically. Hence the researcher should clearly analyse the situation and predictions may be interpreted in his research study.

Tests of Hypothesis

Testing determines the validity of the assumption. The validity of an assumption can be checked through scientific analysis and investigation. Hypothesis testing is based on the basis of sample data nature. But a hypothesis about the population either true or false. Researchers can use the several tests of hypothesis which can be categorised as follows:

(i) Parametric tests
(ii) Non-parametric tests

(i) Parametric tests are related to the parent population aspects. It is based on some assumptions. The observations will collect from a normal population. It is useful for drawing inferences from large samples. It requires less amount of observations. The important parametric tests are presented below for a detailed explanation.

(a) "Z" test
(b) "t" test
(c) Chi-square test
(d) "F" test

(a) Z test is used for various research studies. It is most frequently used test in research studies. It is used for larger sample study. It is related for judging the significance of several statistical measures such as mean. It is used for binomial distribution sample. It is usually for comparison of the mean for sample and population. It is also used to test the significance of **median, mode, coefficient of correlation** etc. It was introduced by **Prof. Fisher**. It is useful to test the significance of the correlation coefficient in small samples. It can be calculated by the following formula:

$$Z = \frac{1}{2} \text{loe}_e \frac{1+r}{1-r}$$

$$Z = 1.1513 \ \log_{10} \left(\frac{1+r}{1-r}\right)$$

$$\xi = \frac{1}{2} \ \log_e \frac{1+P}{1-P} \text{ or } 1.1513 \ \log_{10} \left(\frac{1+P}{1-P}\right)$$

$$\text{Standard normal variate} = \frac{Z-\xi}{1/\sqrt{n-3}}$$

$$\text{S.E.} = \frac{1}{\sqrt{n-3}}$$

Illustration 1: From the following information test the significance of the correlation

r = 0.6 sample size 20
hypothesis correlation = 0.8

Solution: For testing the relation we have to apply z test transformation

$$Z = \frac{1}{2} \ \log_e \ \frac{1+r}{1-r}$$

r = 0.6
P = 0.8
n = 20
or

$$1.1513 \ \log_{10} \frac{1+0.6}{1-0.6} = \frac{1.6}{0.4} = 4$$

$$1.1513 \ \log_4 = 0.6021$$

$$Z = 1.1513 \times 0.6021 = 0.6931$$

$$\xi = \frac{1}{2}\ \log_e \frac{1+P}{1-P}$$

$$= \frac{1}{2}\log_{10}\frac{1+0.8}{1-0.8} = \frac{1.8}{0.2} = 9$$

$$= \frac{1}{2}\log_9 = 1.1513 \times 0.9542 = 1.09$$

difference = $Z - \xi$ 0.6931 – 1.09 = – 0.3969

$$S.E_Z = \frac{1}{\sqrt{20-3}}$$

$$S.E_Z = \frac{1}{\sqrt{17}} = \frac{1}{4.12} = 0.247$$

$$\frac{\text{Difference}}{\text{S.E}} = \frac{-0.3969}{0.247} = -1.60$$

Since the difference is less than 1.96 SE 5% level of significance, it could have arisen due to fluctuations of sampling.

Illustration 2: From the following information calculate z transformation

r = 0.45 sample size 15 hypothesis correlation 0.6

Solution: Applying z transformation, we have to calculate the following measurements: r = 0.45, P = 0.6

$$\frac{\text{Difference}}{\text{S.E}}$$

Difference = $Z - \xi$

$$Z = \frac{1}{2}\log_e \frac{1+r}{1-r} \text{ or } 1.1513 \log \frac{1+0.45}{1-0.45}$$

1.1513 log 2.63 = 0.4200

$\therefore$ Z = 1.1513 × 0.4200 = 0.4835

$$\xi = \frac{1}{2}\log_e \frac{1+P}{1-P}$$

$$= \frac{1}{2}\log_e \frac{1+0.6}{1-0.6}$$

$$= \frac{1}{2}\log_{10} \frac{1.60}{0.4} = 4$$

$$= 1.1513 \times 0.6021 = 0.6931$$

$$\text{SE} = \frac{1}{\sqrt{n-3}} = \frac{1}{\sqrt{15-3}} = \frac{1}{\sqrt{12}} = \frac{1}{3.464} = 0.2886$$

$$\frac{\text{Difference}}{\text{SE}} = \frac{Z-\xi}{\text{SE}}\ \frac{0.4835-0.6931}{0.2886}$$

$$= \frac{-0.2096}{0.2886} = -0.7262$$

Difference is less than 1.96 5 per cent level of significance level.

Illustration 3: From the following information calculate significance level of correlation between sample and observed data

n = 19
r = 0.5
p = 0.4

Solution: Z transformation = Difference/SE

$$\text{Difference} = Z - \xi$$

$$Z = \frac{1}{2}\log_e \frac{1+r}{1-r} \qquad r = 0.5,\ n = 19,\ p = 0.4$$

$$Z = \frac{1}{2} 1.1513 \log_{10} \frac{1+r}{1-r}$$

$$= 1.1513 \log_{10} = \frac{1+0.5}{1-0.5} = \frac{1.5}{0.5} = 3$$

$$= 1.1513 \log_3$$

$$Z = 1.1513 \times 3 = 1.1513 \times 0.4771 = \mathbf{0.5492}$$

$$\xi = \frac{1}{2}\log_e \frac{1+P}{1-P} \qquad P = 0.4$$

$$\frac{1}{2}\log_e \frac{1+0.4}{1-0.4} = \frac{1}{2}\log_e \frac{1.4}{0.6}$$

$$\frac{1}{2}\log_e 2.33$$

$$1.1513 \times 2.33 \log$$

$$1.1513 \times 0.3674 = \mathbf{0.4229}$$

$$SE = \frac{1}{\sqrt{N-3}} = \frac{1}{\sqrt{19-3}} = \frac{1}{\sqrt{16}} = \frac{1}{4} = 0.25$$

$$\text{transformation} = \frac{\text{Difference}}{\text{SE}} = \frac{Z-\xi}{SE}$$

$$\frac{0.5492-0.4229}{0.25} = \frac{0.1263}{0.25} = 0.5052$$

Since difference is less than 2.58 SE (1% level). It may arise due to fluctuations.

Illustration 4: From the following information calculate Fisher's transformation between two samples:

n = 0.5
r = 0.87
n = 12
r = 0.56

Solution: Applying Z text

$$Z = \frac{Z_1 - Z_2}{\sqrt{\frac{1}{n_1-3} + \frac{1}{n_2-3}}}$$

$$Z_1 = \frac{1}{2}\log_e \frac{1+r_1}{1-r_1} \qquad r_1 = 0.87, r_2 = 0.56$$

$$Z_2 = \frac{1}{2}\log_e \frac{1+r_2}{1-r_2} \qquad n_1 = 05, n_2 = 12$$

$$Z_1 = 1.1513\frac{1+0.87}{1-0.87}$$

$$= 1.1513 \log \frac{1.87}{0.13}$$

$$= 1.1513 \log 14.385$$

$$= 1.1513 \times 1.1579 = 1.333$$

$$Z_2 = 1.1513 \times \frac{1+0.56}{1-0.56}$$

$$= 1.1513 \log \frac{1.56}{0.44}$$
$$= 1.1513 \log 3.545$$
$$= 1.1513 \times 0.5496 = 0.6327$$
$$Z_1 – Z_2 = 1.333 – 0.633 = 0.7$$
$$SE_{(Z_1-Z_2)} = \sqrt{\frac{1}{n_1 - 3} + \frac{1}{n_2 - 3}}$$
$$= \sqrt{\frac{1}{5-3} + \frac{1}{12-3}}$$
$$= 0.782$$
$$\frac{Z_1 - Z_2}{SE} = \frac{0.782}{0.782} = 0.895$$

The difference is less than 2.58 (1% level)

Illustration 5: From the following data, test the significance of the difference between two samples by using Fisher's z transformation

Sample size	Correlation
$N_1 = 6$	0.869
$N_2 = 13$	0.551

Solution: Let us take the hypothesis that the samples are drawn from the same population. Applying z-test by the following formula:

$$Z = \frac{Z_1 - Z_2}{\sqrt{\frac{1}{n_1 - 3} + \frac{1}{n_2 - 3}}}$$

$$Z_1 = 1.1513 \log_{10} \frac{1+r_1}{1-r_1}$$

Here $r_1 = 0.869$ $N_1 = 0.6$

$$Z_1 = 1.1513 \log_{10} \frac{1+0.869}{1-0.869}$$
$$= 1.1513 \log \frac{1.869}{0.131}$$
$$= 1.1513 \log 14.267$$
$$= 1.1513 \times 1.1542 = 1.3288$$

$$Z_2 = 1.1513 \log_{10} \frac{1+r_2}{1-r_2}$$

Here $r_2 = 0.551$ $N_2 = 13$

$$Z_2 = 1.1513 \log_{10} \frac{1+0.551}{1-0.551}$$

$$Z_2 = 1.1513 \log_{10} \frac{1.551}{0.449}$$

$$Z_2 = 1.1513 \log 3.4543$$

$$= 1.1513 \times 0.5383 = 0.6197$$

$$Z_1 - Z_2 = 1.3288 - 0.6197 = 0.7091$$

$$SE(Z_1 - Z_2) = \sqrt{\frac{1}{n_1 - 3} + \frac{1}{n_2 - 3}}$$

$$= \sqrt{\frac{1}{6-3} + \frac{1}{13-3}}$$

$$= \sqrt{\frac{1}{3} + \frac{1}{10}}$$

$$= \sqrt{0.33 + 0.1}$$

$$= \sqrt{0.43} = 0.6559$$

$$\therefore \quad \frac{Z_1 - Z_2}{SE} = \frac{0.7091}{0.6559} = 1.0811$$

Hence the difference is less than 2.58 SE (1% level) the experiment provides no evidence against the hypothesis. The samples are drawn from the sample population.

(6) "t" Test: "t" test is very popular. It was introduced by W.S. Gosset. It was developed and submitted in the early 1900. The scientist published his theory with his pen name **"student"**. His findings were published under this name. Afterwards, the "t" distribution became popular. It is based on "t" distribution. It is considered an appropriate test for judging the significance of a sample mean. It is useful to test the significance of means of two samples of small samples when population variance is not known. It can also be used for judging the significance of the coefficients of simple and partial correlations. It is useful for only in case of small samples. It is used when sample size is 30 or less and the population standard deviation is unknown. It can be computed by the following formula:

$$E = \frac{\overline{x} - \mu}{S} \times \sqrt{n}$$

$$S = \sqrt{\frac{E(x - \overline{x})^2}{n - 1}}$$

It ranges from minus infinity to plus infinity. "t" distribution is symmetrical and has a mean zero. It is widely used in practice that samples of size 30 may be considered. It is useful to test the significance of the various results obtained from small samples. The following tests can be judge with the help of "t" distribution:

(a) Significance of the mean of a random sample
(b) Difference between means of two samples (independent)
(c) Difference between means of two samples (dependent)
(d) Observed correlation coefficient

Illustration 6: The electrical manufacturing company produces electric bulbs and supplied to distributors. It claims that its bulbs have a mean life of 26 months with a standard deviation of 6 months. A random sample of 6 bulbs gave the following values:

Life in months 25, 27, 31, 21, 21, 19

Please test the producer's claim at 1% level of significance (table values at degrees of freedom **5, 6 and 7, 4.032, 3.707 and 3.499)**

Solution: Let us assume that there is no significant difference in the mean life of a bulb in the sample and that of the population.

$$t = \left(\frac{\overline{x} - \mu}{s}\right)\sqrt{n}$$

$Z^2 =$ 0.5
$\overline{x} =$ arithmetic mean of the sample
u = population mean/hypothetical mean
n = sample size

s = standard deviation of the sample.

Calculation of Arithmetic mean and standard deviation

x	$x(x-\bar{x})$	x^2
25	–1	1
27	+1	1
31	+5	25
21	–5	25
21	–5	25
19	–7	49
144		126

$$\bar{x} = \frac{\varepsilon X}{n}$$

$$\bar{x} = \frac{144}{6} = 24$$

$$S = \sqrt{\frac{\varepsilon x^2}{n-1}} \qquad Ex^2 = 126$$

$$S = \sqrt{\frac{126}{6-1}}$$

$$S = \sqrt{\frac{126}{5}}$$

$$S = \sqrt{25.2} = 5.01$$

$$t = \left(\frac{\bar{x}-\mu}{S}\right)\sqrt{n} \qquad \bar{x} = 24, \mu = 26$$

$$t = \left(\frac{24-26}{5.01}\right)\sqrt{6} \qquad S = 5.01, n = 6$$

$$t = \frac{2 \times 2.449}{5.01} = 0.9776$$

$v = n - 1 \quad 6 - 1 = 5$ For 5 degrees level of significance 4.032

The calculated value of "t" is less than the Table value. Hence the hypothesis is accepted.

Illustration 7: From the following information calculate "t" test value for the specimen of copper wires.

S.No.	*Strength (in kgs.)*
1.	575
2.	569
3.	567
4.	565
5.	569
6.	575
7.	567
8.	569
9.	593
10.	541

The mean breaking strength of the lot may be taken to be 575 kg. weight test at 5 per cent level of significance.

Applying "t" test, we must find out $\overline{x}$ and standard deviation for the following data:

S.No.	x_i	$x_i - \overline{x}$	$(x_i - \overline{x})^2$
1.	575	+6	36
2.	569	0	0
3.	567	–2	4
4.	565	–4	16
5.	569	0	0
6.	575	+6	36
7.	567	–2	04
8.	569	0	0
9.	593	+24	576
10.	541	–28	784
Ex.	5690		1456

$$\overline{x} = \frac{\varepsilon x}{n} = \frac{5690}{10} = 569 \qquad \overline{x} = 569 \quad \mu = 575$$

$$t = \frac{(\overline{x} - \mu)}{S}\sqrt{n} \qquad n = 10 \quad S = 12.71$$

$$S = \sqrt{\frac{\varepsilon(x_i - \overline{x})^2}{n-1}}$$

$$S = \sqrt{\frac{\varepsilon(1456)}{10-1}}$$

$$S = \sqrt{\frac{1456}{9}}$$

$$S = \sqrt{161.77} = 12.71$$

$$t = \frac{(569 - 575)}{12.71}(\sqrt{10})$$

$$t = \frac{-6}{12.71}(3.16) = -1.49$$

$$t = -1.49$$

Degree of freedom n – 1 = 10 – 1 = 9

5% level of significance at degree of freedom 9, table value is 2.262. It is accepted the null hypothesis.

Illustration 8: Kaveri Restaurant, Mumbai has been having average sales of 600 cups of coffee per day. It expects to increase its sales by some modifications. The daily sales were as follows:

540, 560, 480, 605, 495, 570, 560, 450, 590, 570, 520, 516 on the basis of this sample information, can one conclude that the restaurant sales have increased? Please test the significance at 5 per cent level.

Solution: By applying "t" test

$$t = \frac{\overline{x} - \mu}{S}\sqrt{n}$$

$\overline{x}$ = 538
n = 12
S = 46.68

Arithmetic mean and standard deviation can be computed as follows:

S.No.	x_i	$x_i - \overline{x}$	$(x_i - \overline{x})^2$
1	540	2	04
2	560	22	484
3	480	–58	3364
4	605	67	4489
5	495	–43	1849
6	570	32	1024
7	560	22	484
8	450	–88	7744
9	590	52	2704
10	570	32	1024
11	520	–18	324
12	516	–22	484
Exi	6456		23978

$$\overline{x} = \frac{\varepsilon x_i}{n} = \frac{6456}{12} = 538$$

$$S = \sqrt{\frac{\varepsilon(x_i - \overline{x})^2}{n-1}}$$

$$S = \sqrt{\frac{23978}{12-1}}$$

$$S = \sqrt{\frac{23978}{11}} = \sqrt{2179.81} = 46.68$$

$$t = \frac{\overline{x} - \mu}{S}\sqrt{n}$$

$$t = \frac{538-600}{46.68} \times \sqrt{12}$$

$$t = \frac{-62}{46.68} 3.46$$

$$t = -1.328 \times 3.46 = -4.59$$

Degree of freedom : n – 1 = 12 – 1 = 11

The observed value of t is 3.558. The table value is 1.796. The sample data indicate the restaurants sales have increased.

Illustration 9: The life time of tube lights for a random sample of 10 from a big consignment. The following data is provided for draw inferences.

S.No.	Life span ('000 hours)
1	4.1
2	4.5
3	3.8
4	4.0
5	5.1
6	3.7
7	3.8
8	4.2
9	4.3
10	5.5

Can we accept the hypothesis that the average life time of tube lights is 4100 hours.

Solution: Applying the "t" test

$$t = \frac{\overline{x} - \mu}{S}\sqrt{n}$$

x	$(x - \overline{x})$	$(x - \overline{x})^2$
4.1	–0.2	0.04
4.5	+0.2	0.04
3.8	–0.5	0.25
4.0	–0.3	0.09
5.1	+0.8	0.64
3.7	–0.6	0.36
3.8	–0.5	0.25
4.2	–0.1	0.01
4.3	0	0
5.5	+1.2	1.44
43		3.12

$$\overline{x} = \frac{43}{10} = 4.3$$

$\overline{x} = 4.3 \quad n = 10 \quad \mu = 4.1 \quad S = 0.58$

$$S = \sqrt{\frac{\varepsilon(x - \overline{x})^2}{n-1}} = \sqrt{\frac{3.12}{9}}$$

$$S = \sqrt{0.36} = 0.58$$
$$t = \frac{4.3 - 4.1}{0.58}\sqrt{10}$$
$$t = \frac{0.2 \times 3.162}{0.589} = \frac{0.6324}{0.589} = 1.089$$
$$v = n - 1 = 10 - 1 = 9$$
$$t_{0.05} = 2.262$$

The calculated value of "t" is less than the t able value the hypothesis is accepted.

Illustration 10: The following information is related to drugs. There are two types of drugs provided to patients. These drugs are used for reducing their weight. Drug x was imported and drug y is available in domestic market. The decrease in the weight after using the drugs for 8 months was as follows:

Drug x	*Drug y*
11	9
13	10
14	13
12	15
15	16
	11
	10

You are required to recommend which drug should we buy. Table value v = 10 $t_{0.05} = 2.223$

Solution: Let us take the hypothesis that there is no significant difference in the efficacy of two drugs. Applying t test

$$t = \frac{\overline{x}_1 - \overline{x}_2}{S}\sqrt{\frac{n_1 - n_2}{n_1 + n_2}}$$

$\overline{x}_1 = 12$ $\qquad \overline{x}_2 = 12$

$n_1 = 05$ $\qquad n_2 = 07$

x_1	dx	dx^2	x_2	dy	dy^2
11	–1	1	9	–3	9
13	0	0	10	–2	4
14	+2	4	13	0	0
12	0	0	15	+2	4
15	+3	9	16	+3	9
Ex = 65		14	11	–2	4
			10	–3	9
			Ex 84		39

$$\overline{x} = \frac{\varepsilon x}{n} = \frac{65}{5} = 13$$

$$\overline{x} = \frac{\varepsilon x}{n} = \frac{84}{7} = 12$$

$$\overline{x} = 13 \quad \overline{x}_2 = 12 \quad n_1 = 5 \quad n_2 = 7$$

$$t = \frac{\overline{x}_1 - \overline{x}_2}{S}\sqrt{\frac{n_1 - n_2}{n_1 + n_2}}$$

$$S = \sqrt{\frac{\varepsilon(x_1 - x_1)^2 + \varepsilon(x_2 - \overline{x}_2)^2}{n_1 + n_2 - 2}}$$

$$S = \sqrt{\frac{14 + 39}{5 + 7 - 2}}$$

$$S = \sqrt{\frac{53}{10}} = \sqrt{5.3}$$

$$S = 2.30$$

$$t = \frac{13 - 12}{2.30}\sqrt{\frac{5 \times 7}{5 + 7}}$$

$$t = \frac{1}{2.30}\sqrt{\frac{35}{12}}$$

$$t = \frac{1}{2.30} \times 1.70$$

$$t = 0.43 \times 1.70 = \mathbf{0.739}$$

$$v = n_1 + n_2 - 2 = 5 + 7 - 2 = 10 \; t_{0.05} = 2.228$$

The calculated value of "t" is less than the table value. The hypothesis is accepted. It is recommended that drugs y should be purchased.

Illustration 11: The following information is related to diet programme of 10 persons. The diet "x" is served to 10 persons. Another diet is served to 12 members of "y".

diet x : 11, 7, 17, 18, 14, 13, 9, 15, 16, 10
diet y : 8, 14, 23, 16, 13, 15, 19, 9, 22, 24, 11, 18

test whether the diet which influence the weight of persons degree of freedom at 5% level of significance.

19 – 2.09, 20 – 2.09, 21 – 2.08, 22 – 2.07, 23 – 2.07.

Solution: Let us take the null hypothesis that the diets do not differ significantly. Applying "t" test:

$$t = \frac{\bar{x}_1 - \bar{x}_2}{S}\sqrt{\frac{n_1 n_2}{n_1 + n_2}}$$

$\bar{x}_1 = 13 \quad \bar{x}_2 = 17 \quad n_1 = 10 \quad n_2 = 12$

$$S = \sqrt{\frac{(\varepsilon dx)^2 + (\varepsilon dy)^2}{n_1 + n_2 - 2}}$$

drug x	*dx*	*dx²*	*drug y*	*dy*	*dy²*
11	–2	4	8	–9	81
7	–6	36	14	–3	9
17	+4	16	23	+6	36
18	+5	25	16	–1	1
14	+1	01	13	–4	16
13	0	0	15	–2	4
9	–4	16	19	+2	4
15	+2	4	9	–8	64
16	+3	9	22	+5	25
10	–3	9	24	+7	49
			12	–5	25
			19	+2	4
130		120	204		318

$$\bar{x} = \frac{\varepsilon dx}{n} = \frac{130}{10} = 13$$

$$\bar{y} = \frac{\varepsilon dxy}{n} = \frac{204}{12} = 17$$

$$S = \sqrt{\frac{\varepsilon dx^2 + \varepsilon dy^2}{n_1 + n_2 - 2}}$$

$$S = \sqrt{\frac{120 + 318}{10 + 12 - 2}}$$

$$S = \sqrt{\frac{438}{20}} = \sqrt{\frac{438}{20}} = \sqrt{21.9} = 4.67$$

$$t = \sqrt{\frac{13 - 17}{4.66}} \times \sqrt{\frac{10 \times 12}{10 + 12}}$$

$$t = \frac{4}{4.66} \times 2.34$$

$$t = 2.00$$

$$V = n_1 + n_2 - 2 \quad 10 + 12 - 2 = 20$$

20 degrees of freedom table value of t at 5 per cent level is 2.09. The calculated value is less than the table value and diets do not differ significantly.

Illustration 12: Two famous laboratories x and y carry out an experiment regarding ice-cream made by a company. The experiment is related to fat content in ice-cream. The sample is supplied to these laboratories and the content was found as below:

Batch No.	*Lab x*	*Lab y*
1	9	11
2	10	10
3	9	10
4	5	06
5	10	09
6	8	09
7	11	11
8	6	08
9	9	08
10	10	08

is there a significant difference between the mean fat content obtained by the two laboratories

Degrees of freedom	*5% value of t*
6	1.45
7	2.36
8	2.31
9	2.26
10	2.23
16	2.12
18	2.10
20	2.09

Solution: Let us take hypothesis that there is no significant difference. The mean content obtained by the laboratories. Applying "t" test

$$t = \frac{\bar{x}_1 - \bar{x}_2}{S} \times \sqrt{\frac{n_1 n_2}{n_1 + n_2}}$$

First we have to find out mean, standard deviation for the given data.

Batch No.	X_1	*(Ax=8)* *dx*	dx^2	*y*	*(Ay=9)* *Dy*	dy^2
1.	9	+1	1	11	+2	4
2.	10	+2	4	10	+1	1
3.	9	+1	1	10	+1	1
4.	5	-3	9	06	-3	9
5.	10	+2	4	09	0	0
6.	8	0	0	09	0	0
7.	11	+3	9	11	+2	4
8.	06	-2	4	08	-1	1
9.	09	+1	1	08	-1	1
10.	10	+2	4	08	-1	1
		+12	37		+6	22
		–5			–6	
		+7			0	

Since the actual means are in fraction, we shall take deviations from the assumed mean.

$$\bar{x}_1 = Ax + \frac{dx}{n} = 8 + \frac{7}{10} \qquad \bar{y} = Ay + \frac{\varepsilon dy}{n}$$

$$\bar{x} = 8 + 0.7 = 8.7 \qquad 9 + \frac{0}{10} = 9$$

$$S = \sqrt{\frac{\varepsilon(x_1 - A_1)^2 + \varepsilon(x_2 - A_2)^2 - n_1(\bar{x}_1 - A_1)^2 - n_2(\bar{x}_2 - A_2)^2}{n_1 + n_2 - 2}}$$

$$= \sqrt{\frac{\varepsilon(37) + 22 - 10(8.7 - 8)^2 - 10(9 - 9)^2}{10 + 10 - 2}}$$

$$= \sqrt{\frac{59 - 4.9 - 0}{18}}$$

$$= \sqrt{\frac{54.1}{18}} = \sqrt{3.05} = 1.734$$

$\bar{x}_1 = 8.7 \quad \bar{x}_2 = 9 \quad n_1 = 10 \quad n_2 = 10.5 = 1.734$

$$t = \frac{x_1 - x_2}{S} \times \sqrt{\frac{n_1 n_2}{n_1 + n_2}}$$

$$t = \frac{8.7 - 9}{1.734} \times \sqrt{\frac{10 \times 10}{10 + 10}}$$

$$t = \frac{0.3}{1.734} \times \sqrt{\frac{100}{20}}$$

$$t = \frac{0.3}{1.734} \times 2.236$$

$$t = 0.173 \times 2.236 = 0.39$$

$$v = n_1 + n_2 - 2 = 10 + 10 - 2 = 18$$

For $v = 18$ $t_{0.05} = 2.10$

Since the hypothesis value is less than the table value, the mean fat content obtained by these laboratories do not differ significantly.

Illustration 13: The following data is related to marks secured by a different group of students. Examine the significance of difference between mean of the marks secured by two groups.

"t" value at 5% level of significance level V = 14 is 2.14

Group "a"	*Group "b"*
20	31
22	30
38	28
52	37
51	32
38	46
36	48
51	
43	

Solution: Let us take hypothesis that there is no significant difference in the mean of marks secured by two groups applying "t" test:

$$t = \frac{\overline{x}_1 - \overline{x}_2}{S}\sqrt{\frac{n_1 n_2}{n_1 + n_2}}$$

Group "a" x_1	$(x_1 - \overline{x}_1)$	$(x_1 - \overline{x})^2$	*Group "b"* x_2	$(x_2 - \overline{x}_2)^2$ $\overline{x}_2$	$(x_2 - \overline{x}_2)^2$
20	–19	361	31	–5	25
22	–17	289	30	–6	36
38	–01	1	28	–8	64
52	+13	169	37	+1	1
51	+12	144	32	–4	16
38	–1	1	46	+10	100
36	–3	9	48	+12	144
51	+12	144	—	—	—
43	+4	16	—	—	—
351	+41	1134	252	0	386
—	-41	—	—	—	—
—	0	—	—	—	—

$$\overline{x}_1 = \frac{ex_1}{n} \qquad \overline{x}_2 = \frac{252}{7} = 36$$

$$\overline{x}_1 = \frac{351}{9} = 39$$

$$S = \sqrt{\frac{\varepsilon(x_1 - \overline{x}_1)^2 + \varepsilon(x_2 - \overline{x}_2)^2}{n_1 + n_2 - 2}}$$

$$S = \sqrt{\frac{1134 + 386}{9 + 7 - 2}}$$

$$S = \sqrt{\frac{1520}{14}} = 10.42$$

$$t = \frac{39 - 36}{10.42}\sqrt{\frac{9 \times 7}{9 + 7}}$$

$$= \frac{3}{10.42}\sqrt{\frac{63}{16}}$$

$$= \frac{3}{10.42} \times 1.984 = 0.571$$

$$t_{0.05} = 2.14$$

Calculated value is less than the table value and hypothesis holds true.

Illustration 14: The following information is related to the performance of 12 students in an examination of accountancy paper. The impact is as follows:

Roll No.	*Before Coaching*	*After Coaching*
1	46	55
2	42	40
3	63	71
4	54	59
5	34	48
6	46	41
7	72	75
8	43	50
9	69	75
10	74	76
11	55	62
12	74	80

Solution: Let us take the hypothesis that there is no difference in the marks obtained before and after coaching.

$$\varepsilon = \frac{\bar{d}\sqrt{n}}{S}$$

Roll No.	Before coaching	After coaching	(After-before) coaching d	d^2
1.	46	55	+9	81
2.	42	40	-2	04
3.	63	71	+8	64
4.	54	59	+5	25
5.	34	48	+14	196
6.	46	41	-5	25
7.	72	75	+3	09
8.	43	50	+7	49
9.	69	75	+6	36
10.	74	76	+2	04
11.	55	62	+7	49
12.	74	80	+6	36
			Ed = 60	Ed^r = 578

$$\bar{d} = \frac{\varepsilon d}{n}\ \frac{60}{12} = 5 \qquad \bar{d} = 2\ \ n = 12\ \ S = 5.03$$

$$S = \sqrt{\frac{\varepsilon d^2 - n(\bar{d})^2}{n-1}} \qquad t = \frac{\bar{d}\sqrt{n}}{S}$$

$$S = \sqrt{\frac{578 - 12(5)^2}{12-1}} \qquad t = \frac{5 \times \sqrt{12}}{5.03}$$

$$S = \sqrt{\frac{578 - 12(25)}{11}} \qquad t = \frac{5 \times 3.46}{5.03}$$

$$S = \sqrt{\frac{578 - 300}{11}} \qquad t = \frac{17.3}{5.03} = 3.43$$

$$S = \sqrt{\frac{278}{11}} = 5.03$$

$v = n - 1 \quad 12 - 1 = 11 \qquad v = 11 \quad t_{0.05} = 2.201$

The calculated value of "t" is more than the table value. Hence hypothesis is rejected. Therefore the coaching has been useful to the students.

Illustration 15: The following information is related to 10 patients. They are taking treatment for blood pressure. A drug is served their and pressure were recorded as follows:

5, 8, –4, 6, –5, 6, 2, 2, 4

Examine whether the drug has no effect on change of blood pressure? (5% value of t for 9 d.f. 2.26%)

Solution: Let us take hypothesis that the drug has no effect on change of blood pressure. Applying "t" test

$$t = \frac{\bar{d}\sqrt{n}}{S}$$

$$d = \frac{\varepsilon d}{n} \qquad S = \sqrt{\frac{\varepsilon d^2 - n(\bar{d})^2}{n-1}}$$

d	*d*²
5	25
8	64
–4	16
6	36
–5	25
6	36
2	4
2	4
4	16
+33	Ed² 226
–9	
Ed +24	

$$\bar{d} = \frac{\varepsilon d^2}{n} = \frac{24}{9} = 2.66$$

$$S = \sqrt{\frac{\varepsilon d^2 - n(\bar{d})^2}{n-1}}$$

$$S = \sqrt{\frac{226 - 10(2.6)^2}{9-1}}$$

$$S = \sqrt{\frac{226 - 10(6.76)}{8}}$$

$$S = \sqrt{\frac{226 - 67.6}{8}}$$

$$S = \sqrt{\frac{158.4}{8}}$$

$$S = \sqrt{17.61} = 4.44$$

$\bar{d} = 2.4$ $\quad\quad$ $S = 4.49$ $\quad\quad$ $n = 9$

$$t = \frac{2.66\sqrt{9}}{4.44}$$

$$t = \frac{2.66 \times 3}{4.44} = \frac{7.98}{4.44} = 1.78$$

The calculated value is less than the table value. The hypothesis is accepted. Hence the drug has no effect on the blood pressure.

Illustration 16: The following information is related to 10 couples regarding age at marriage. Find the correlation coefficient and test for its significance.

Husband's age	*Wife's age*
26	21
30	25
31	26
32	27
33	28
34	29
36	31
38	32
39	33
42	35

Solution: Let us take the hypothesis that there is no correlation between husband and wife age.

Applying t test $= \dfrac{r \ x}{\sqrt{1-r^2}} \sqrt{n-2}$

Let us first calculate correlation between pairs

x	*dx*	*dx²*	*y*	*dy*	*dy²*	*dx-dy*
26	0	0	21	0	0	0
30	+4	16	25	+4	16	16
31	+5	25	26	+5	25	25
32	+6	36	27	+6	36	36
33	+7	49	28	+7	49	49
34	+8	64	29	+8	64	64
36	+10	100	31	+10	100	100
38	+12	144	32	+12	121	132
39	+13	169	33	+12	144	156
42	+16	256	35	+14	196	224
	81	859		77	751	802

$$r = \frac{n \times \varepsilon dx.dy - (\varepsilon dx)(\varepsilon dy)}{\sqrt{n \times \varepsilon dx^2 - (\varepsilon dx)^2} \times \sqrt{N \times \varepsilon dy^2 - (dy)^2}}$$

$$r = \frac{10 \times 802 - (81)(77)}{\sqrt{10 \times 859 - (81)^2} \times \sqrt{10 \times 751 - (77)^2}}$$

$$r = \frac{8020 - 6237}{\sqrt{8590 - (6561)} \times \sqrt{7510 - 5929}}$$

$$r = \frac{1783}{\sqrt{2029} \times \sqrt{1581}}$$

$$r = \frac{1783}{45.04 \times 39.76}$$

$$r = \frac{1783}{1790.79} = 0.99$$

$$r = 0.99$$

$$t = \frac{0.99}{\sqrt{1-(.99)^2}} \times \sqrt{10-2}$$

$$t = \frac{0.99 \times 2.82}{\sqrt{1 - 0.9801}}$$

$$t = \frac{0.99 \times 2.82}{0.14106}$$

$$t = \frac{2.7918}{0.14106} = 19.79$$

$v = n - 2$ $\quad 10 - 2 = 8$ $\quad t_{0.05} = 2.31$

Calculated value is more than the table value. Hence the hypothesis is accepted. The correlation is significant.

Illustration 17: The following information is related to a random selection of 10 workers in a factory. The produced items are:

55, 56, 57, 59, 60, 61, 62, 63, 63, 64

The population mean is 59. Test the significance of the mean of the given data (5% value of t for 9 d.f. is 2.262)

Solution: Let us first calculate the sample mean and standard deviation applying t test.

$$t = \frac{\overline{x} - \mu}{S}\sqrt{n}$$

x	*dx*	*dx*²
55	–5	25
56	–4	16
57	–3	9
59	–1	1
60	0	0
61	+1	1
62	+2	4
63	+3	9
63	+3	9
64	+4	16
Ex 600		90

$$x = \frac{\varepsilon x}{n} = \frac{600}{10} = 60$$

$$S = \sqrt{\frac{\varepsilon(x - \overline{x})^2}{n-1}}$$

$$S = \sqrt{\frac{90}{10-9}}$$

$$S = \sqrt{\frac{90}{9}} = \sqrt{10} = 3.162$$

$$t = \frac{60-59}{3.162} \times \sqrt{10}$$

$$t = \frac{1}{3.162} \times 3.162 = 1 \qquad t_{00.5} = 2.262$$

The calculated value is less than the table value hypothesis is accepted.

Illustration 18: The following information is related to six randomly chosen from army are in inches 79, 73, 71, 72, 72, 71. Another 6 members randomly selected from Navy are 71, 67, 68, 72, 75, 67. The Army is taller than Navy do you agree? Use "t" test.

Solution: Let us take the hypothesis that there is no difference in height from Army and Navy applying "t" test.

$$t = \frac{\overline{x}_1 - \overline{x}_2}{S} \sqrt{\frac{n_1 n_2}{n_1 + n_2}}$$

x_1	$(x_1 - \overline{x}_1)$	$(x_1 - \overline{x}_1)^2$	x_2	$(x_2 - \overline{x}_2)$	$(x_2 - x_2)^2$
79	+6	36	71	+1	1
73	0	0	67	-3	9
71	-2	4	68	-2	4
72	-1	1	72	+2	4
72	-1	1	75	+5	25
71	-2	4	67	-3	9
438	-6	46	420	-8	52
	+6			+8	
	0			0	

$$\bar{x}_1 = \frac{438}{6} = 73 \qquad \bar{x}_2 = \frac{420}{6} = 70$$

$$S = \sqrt{\frac{\varepsilon(x_1 - x_2)^2 + \varepsilon(x_2 - \bar{x}_2)^2}{n_1 + n_2 - 2}}$$

$$S = \sqrt{\frac{46 + 52}{6 + 6 - 2}}$$

$$S = \sqrt{\frac{98}{10}} = \sqrt{9.8} = 3.130$$

$$t = \frac{73 - 70}{3.13}\sqrt{\frac{6 \times 6}{6 + 6}}$$

$$\frac{3}{3.13} \times 1.732 = 1.66$$

Calculated value is less than table value.

Illustration 19: The following information is related to sales of a company. The company undertakes an advertising campaign for increasing the sales volume. The data collected from 6 retail outlets of the company.

Shops No.	*Before advertising campaign*	*After advertising campaign*
1	55	60
2	30	31
3	33	32
4	50	57
5	52	58
6	44	47

Test the advertising campaign impact on sales of a company test the analysis at 5% level of significance.

Solution: Let us take hypothesis that advertising campaign has not been a success. Applying "t" test

$$t = \frac{\bar{d}\sqrt{n}}{S}$$

Shop No.	*Before ad. campaign*	*After ad. campaign*	*d*	*d²*
1	55	60	+5	25
2	30	31	+1	1
3	33	32	–1	1
4	50	57	+7	49
5	52	58	+6	36
6	44	47	+3	09
			+22	121
			-01	
			+21	

$$\bar{d} = \frac{\varepsilon d}{n} = \frac{21}{6} = 3.50$$

$$S = \sqrt{\frac{\varepsilon d^2 - n(\bar{d})^2}{n-1}}$$

$$S = \sqrt{\frac{121 - 6(3.5)^2}{6-1}}$$

$$S = \sqrt{\frac{121 - 6(12.25)}{5}}$$

$$S = \sqrt{\frac{121 - 73.5}{5}}$$

$$S = \sqrt{\frac{47.5}{5}} = \sqrt{9.5} = 3.08$$

$$v = n - 1 = 6 - 1 = 5$$

$$t = \frac{\bar{d}\sqrt{n}}{S} \qquad \bar{d} = 3.50, n = 5, S = 3.08$$

$$t = \frac{3.5\sqrt{6}}{3.08}$$

$$t = \frac{3.5 \times 2.44}{3.08}$$

$$t = \frac{8.54}{3.08} = 2.77 \qquad t_{0.05} = 2.57$$

The calculated value is greater than the table value. The null hypothesis is rejected. The advertising campaign has been successful.

Illustration 20: Slimwell, an obsity agency conducting a weight reduction programme. The agency claims that it has achieved a weight reduction of at least 5 kgs. after two weeks of the programme. The data is provided 10 participants who had undergone this programme.

Before Programme (Kgs.)	*Weight after programme (Kgs.)*
89	80
95	87
103	95
96	90
91	83
83	77
91	83
95	88
98	98
109	99

test at a significance level of 5%.

Solution: Let us take the null hypothesis that the programme does not show an impact on weight reduction of the participant. Applying "t" test

$$t = \frac{\bar{d}\sqrt{n}}{S}$$

Before Programme	*After Programme*	*d*	*d²*
89	80	–9	81
95	87	–8	64
103	95	–8	64
96	90	–6	36
91	83	–8	64
83	77	–6	36
91	83	–8	64
95	88	–7	49
98	98	0	0
109	99	–10	100
		70	558

$$\bar{d} = \frac{\varepsilon d}{n} = \frac{70}{10} = 7$$

$$S = \sqrt{\frac{\varepsilon d^2 - n(\bar{d})^2}{n-1}}$$

$$S = \sqrt{\frac{558 - 10(-7)^2}{10-1}}$$

$$S = \sqrt{\frac{558 - 10(49)}{9}}$$

$$S = \sqrt{\frac{558 - 490}{9}}$$

$$S = \sqrt{\frac{68}{9}} = \sqrt{7.55} = 2.74$$

$$t = \frac{7 \times \sqrt{10}}{2.77} = \frac{7 \times 3.16}{2.77} = \frac{22.13}{2.77} = 7.99$$

$v = n - 1 = 10 - 1 = 9$ $\qquad\qquad t_{0.05} = 2.28$

Calculated value is greater than the table value. Hence the hypothesis is rejected. The weight reduction programme conducted by the agency has been successful.

Illustration 21: The following information is related to Asia Brown Bravery Ltd. The company appointed 10 sales persons in the marketing department. Their performance was recorded. Their means sale was noted. All these newly appointed persons were provided with 6 months training programme to stimulate their abilities. Their performance were presented below:

Employees Code No.	*Before training*	*After training*
101	30	31
102	25	25
103	40	39
104	20	18
105	47	48
106	33	45

Employees Code No.	*Before training*	*After training*
107	31	34
108	49	46
109	40	41
110	53	51

By applying "t" test, test the significance of the training programme? 5% level of significance.

Solution: Let us take the null hypothesis that the training programme have not benefited to the employees. Applying "t" test.

Before training	*After training*	*d (after – before)*	*d^2*
30	31	+1	1
25	25	0	0
40	39	–1	1
20	18	–2	4
47	48	+1	1
33	45	+12	144
31	34	+3	9
49	46	–3	9
40	41	+1	1
53	51	–2	4
		10	174

$$t = \frac{\bar{d}\sqrt{n}}{S} \qquad \bar{d} = \frac{\varepsilon \bar{d}}{n} = \frac{10}{10} = 1 \qquad n = 10$$

$$S = \sqrt{\frac{\varepsilon d^2 - n(\bar{d})^2}{n-1}}$$

$$S = \sqrt{\frac{174 - 10(1)^2}{10-1}}$$

$$S = \sqrt{\frac{174-10}{9}} = \sqrt{\frac{164}{9}} = 4.26$$

$$t = \frac{1 \times \sqrt{10}}{4.26} = 0.741$$

$v = n - 1 \qquad 10 - 1 = 9 \qquad t_{0.05} = 2.262$

The calculated value is less than the table value. Hence hypothesis is accepted. The training programme has been useful to the employees.

(c) Chi-square test: Chi-square test is one of the important parametric test. Parametric test contains the values of population. Hence it is known as **"parametric tests"**. The testing procedure requires assumption about the kind of population. X^2 test based on chi-square distribution. The parametric test is used for comparing a sample variance to a theoretical population variance. A detailed discussion is available in the forthcoming chapters.

(d) "F" test: "F" test is also called as Analysis of Variance **(ANOVA).** F test is based as "F" distribution. It is used to compare the variance of the two independent samples. It is used for judging the significance of more than two sample means at one and the same time. It is calculated and compared with its probable value for accepting or rejecting the null hypothesis. It is also useful to test the equality of variances of two normal populations. "F" test can be computed by the following formula:

$$F = \frac{\sigma_1^2}{\sigma_2^2}$$

$$\sigma_1^2 = \frac{\varepsilon(x_1 - \bar{x}_1)^2}{(n_1 - 1)}$$

$$\sigma_2^2 = \frac{\varepsilon(x_{2i} - \bar{x}_2)^2}{(n_2 - 1)}$$

$$F = \frac{\text{Larger estimate of variance}}{\text{Smaller estimate of variance}}$$

$v_1 = n_1 - 1 \qquad v_2 = n_2 - 1$

Illustration 22: From the following information test whether the populations have the same variance at the 5% level of significance (F = 3.36) 5% $V_1 = 10$ $V_2 = 9$.

The random samples were drawn from two normal populations and their values.

X	*Y*
70	68
71	70
79	78
80	82
86	86
88	89
92	91
94	96
96	97
	99
	101

Solution: Let us take hypothesis that the two populations have the same variance applying "t" test.

$$F = \frac{S_1^2}{S_2^2}$$

x	*Ex*	*Ex²*	*y*	*Ey*	*Ey²*
70	–14	196	68	–19	361
71	–13	169	70	–17	289
79	–05	25	78	–9	81
80	–04	16	82	–5	25
86	+2	04	86	–1	1
88	+4	16	89	+2	4
92	+8	64	91	+4	16
94	+10	100	96	+9	81
96	+12	144	97	+10	100
			99	+12	144
			101	+14	196
756	Ex = 0	734	957	εy = 0	1298

$$\bar{x} = \frac{\varepsilon x}{n} = \frac{756}{9} = 84 \qquad \bar{y} = \frac{\varepsilon y}{n} = \frac{957}{11} = 87$$

$$S_1^2 = \frac{\varepsilon y^2}{n-1} = \frac{734}{9-1} = 91.75$$

$$S_2^2 = \frac{\varepsilon y^2}{n-1} = \frac{1298}{11-1} = \frac{1298}{10} = 129.8$$

$$F = \frac{129.8}{91.75} = 1.414$$

For $v_1 = 10$ and $v_2 = 8$ $F_{0.05} = 3.36$

The calculated value of "F" is less than the table value. The hypothesis is accepted. It may be calculated that the two populations have the same variance.

Illustration 23: From the following data test whether the two samples have the same variance at 5 per cent level of significance. The samples are drawn from two normal populations.

Sample A	*Sample B*
65	66
70	71
76	72
79	90
81	83
87	68
90	90
92	91
	93
	96

Solution: Let us take the hypothesis that the two populations have the same variance. Applying "t" test

Sample A (x)	*x*	*x^2*	*Sample B (y)*	*y*	*y^2*
65	–15	225	66	–16	256
70	–10	100	71	–11	121
76	–04	16	72	–10	100
79	–01	1	90	+8	64
81	+1	1	83	+1	1

(*Contd.*)

(*Contd.*)

Sample A (*x*)	*x*	x^2	*Sample B* (*y*)	*y*	y^2
87	+7	49	68	–14	196
90	+10	100	90	+8	64
92	+12	144	91	+9	81
			93	+11	121
			96	+14	196
640		636	830		1200

$$\overline{x} = \frac{\varepsilon x}{n} = \frac{640}{8} = 80 \qquad \overline{y} = \frac{820}{n} = \frac{820}{10} = 82$$

$$S_1^2 = \frac{\varepsilon x^2}{n_1 - 1} = \frac{636}{8-1} = \frac{636}{7} = 90.85$$

$$S_2^2 = \frac{\varepsilon x^2}{n_2 - 1} = \frac{1200}{10-1} = \frac{1200}{9} = 133.33$$

$$F = \frac{133.33}{90.857} = 1.468$$

For $v_1 = 9, v_2 = 7, F_{0.05} = 3.68$

The calculated value of F is less than the table value. The hypothesis holds good. We conclude that the two populations have the same variance.

Illustration 24: The following information is related to business schools in Mumbai. A common test was conducted to a number of students at random from the final semester of each of the four Business schools concerned. The results are given below. You are required to analyse the variance of data.

Business Schools

A	B	C	D
11	15	21	16
13	14	15	12
15	12	19	15
11	17	09	19
10	07	11	18

Solution: Let us assume business schools A, B, C, D is a x_1, x_2, x_3, x_4.

x_1	x_1^2	x_2	x_2^2	x_3	x_3^2	x_4	x_4^2
11	121	15	225	21	441	16	256
13	169	14	196	15	225	12	144
15	225	12	144	19	361	15	225
11	121	17	289	9	81	19	361
10	100	7	49	11	121	18	324
60	736	65	903	75	1229	80	1310

Sum of all the items of various samples: 60+65+75+80 = 280

$$\text{Correction factor} = \frac{T^2}{n} = \frac{280^2}{20}$$

$$= \frac{78400}{20} = 3920$$

Total sum of squares

$$= \varepsilon x_1^{\ 2} + \varepsilon x_2^{\ 2} + \varepsilon x_3^{\ 2} + \varepsilon x_4^{\ 2} - \frac{T^2}{N}$$

$$= 736 + 903 + 1229 + 1310 - 3920$$

$$= 4178 - 3920 = 258$$

Sum of squares between the samples

$$= \frac{(\varepsilon x_1)^2}{n} + \frac{(\varepsilon x_2)^2}{n} + \frac{(\varepsilon x_3)^2}{n} + \frac{(\varepsilon x_4)^2}{n} - \frac{T^2}{N}$$

$$= \frac{(60)^2}{5} + \frac{(65)^2}{5} + \frac{(75)^2}{5} + \frac{(80)^2}{5} - 3920$$

$$= \frac{3600}{5} + \frac{4225}{5} + \frac{5625}{5} + \frac{6400}{5} - 3920$$

$$= \frac{19850}{5} - 3920$$

$$= 3970 - 3920 = 50$$

Sum of squares within sampls = Total sum of squares – sum of squares beween samples

$$= 258 - 50 = 208$$

Variation	*Sum of squares*	*Degrees of freedom*	*Mean Square*
between samples	50	3	$50 \div 3 = 16.7$
within samples	208	16	$208 \div 16 = 13$
	258	19	

The table value of F for $V_1 = 3$ $V_2 = 16$ at 15% level of significance is 3.24. The calculated value of "F" is less than table value and hence the difference in the mean values of the sample is not significant.

$$F = \frac{\text{Variance between samples}}{\text{Variance within samples}} = \frac{16.7}{13} = 1.285$$

Illustration 25: The following information is related to a company's monthly sales of three states by its regional sales managers.

States	*RSM I*	*RSM II*	*RSM III*	*RSM IV*
A.P.	10	9	7	12
Tamilnadu	12	14	10	9
Karnataka	14	11	12	11

Draw the analysis of variance and test whether there is any significant difference between sales by the regional sales managers and between three states.

Solution: Let us take hypothesis that there is a significant differences between the sales by the regional sales managers and there is no significant difference between sales in three states.

States	*RSM I*	*RSM II*	*RSM III*	*RSM IV*	*Total*
A.P.	10	9	7	12	38
Tamilnadu	12	14	10	9	45
Karnataka	14	11	12	11	48
	36	34	29	32	131
$\bar{x}$	12	11.33	9.66	10.66	

$$\text{Correction factor} = \frac{T^2}{N} = \frac{(131)^2}{12}$$

$$= \frac{17161}{12} = 1430.08$$

Total sum of squares $(10)^2 + (12)^2 + (14)^2 + (9)^2 + (14)^2 + (11)^2 + (7)^2 + (10)^2 + (12)^2 + (12)^2 + (9)^2 + (11)^2$

$= 100 + 144 + 196 + 81 + 196 + 121 + 49 + 100 + 144 + 144 + 81 + 121 = 1477$

$= 1477 - 1430.08 = 46.92$

Sum of squares between RSM

$$= \frac{1}{3}[(36)^2 + (34)^2 + (29)^2 + (32)^2] - CF$$

$$= \frac{1}{3}(1296 + 1156 + 841 + 1024) - 1430.08$$

$$= \frac{1}{3}(4317) - 1430.08$$

$= 1439 - 1430.08 = 8.92$

Sum of squares between RSM (rows)

$$= \frac{1}{4} \times (38^2 + 45^2 + 48^2) - CF$$

$$= \frac{1}{4}(1444 + 2025 + 2304) - 1430.08$$

$$= \frac{1}{4}(5773) - 1430.08 = 1443.25 - 1430.08 = 13.17$$

RE $= TSS - SSC - SSR$

$= 46.92 - 8.92 - 13.17$

RE $= 24.83$

ANOVA TABLE

Sources of variation	*Sum of squares*	*Degrees of freedom*	*Mean square*
Between columns	8.92	3	2.970
Between rows	13.17	2	6.585
Residual	24.83	6	4.138
	46.92	11	

$$F = \frac{2.97}{4.138} = 0.717$$

For $V_1 = 3$ $V_1 = 5$ $F_{0.05} = 4.76$ the calculated value is less than table value. The sales of different regional sales managers do not differ significantly.

There the state variance

$$F = \frac{6.585}{4.138} = 1.59$$

For $V_1 = V_2 = 6$ $F_{0.05} = 4.76$ the calculated value is less than the table value. Hence there is no significant difference in the states as far as sales is concerned.

Illustration 26: The following information is related to test scores of CAT. The students are belonging to Mumbai, Delhi and Kolkata. Their scores were found as follows:

	SCORES				
Mumbai	100	80	70	60	90
Delhi	80	50	60	50	60
Kolkata	70	60	70	80	70

Perform analysis of variance and show if there is any significant differences between the test scores of students in Metropolitan Cities (F% 3.44)

Solution:

Mumbai	x_1^2	*Delhi*	x_2^2	*Kolkata*	x_3^2
100	10,000	80	6,400	70	4,900
80	6,400	50	2,500	60	3,600
70	4,900	60	3,600	70	4,900
60	3,600	50	2,500	80	6,400
90	8,100	60	3,600	70	4,900
400	33,000	300	18,600	350	24,700

The sum of all items of samples $ex_1 + ex_2 + ex_3$

$400 + 300 + 350 = 1050$

Correction factor = $\frac{T^2}{N}\ \frac{1050^2}{15} = \frac{1102500}{15} = 73500$

Total sum of squares

$= \varepsilon x_1{}^2 + \varepsilon x_2{}^2 + \varepsilon x_3{}^2 - \frac{T^2}{N}$

$= 33000 + 18600 + 24700 - 73.500$

$= 76300 - 73.500 = 2800$

Sum of squares between the samples

$= \frac{(ex_1)^2}{n} + \frac{(ex_2)^2}{n} + \frac{(ex_3)^2}{n} - \frac{T^2}{N}$

$\frac{160000}{5} + \frac{90000}{5} + \frac{122500}{5} - 73500$

$= \frac{372500 - 73500}{5}$

$= 74500 - 73500 = 1000$

Mean sum of squares between the samples $\frac{1000}{2} = 500$

$$\frac{d}{b} 3 - 1 = 2$$

Sum of squares within samples total = sum of squares – Sum of squares between samples

$= 2800 - 1000 = 1800$

Mean sum of squares within the samples

$= \frac{1800}{15-3} = \frac{1800}{12} = 150$

Variation	*Sum of squares*	*s/f*	*Mean squares*
between samples	1000	2	500
within samples	1800	12	150
	2800	14	650

$$F = \frac{\text{Variance between samples}}{\text{Variance within samples}} = \frac{500}{150} = 3.33$$

The calculated value of F is less than the critical value. The samples could have come from the same universe.

Illustration 27: From the following information perform a two way ANOVA on the data given below.

Plots	A	B	C	D
	Treatment			
I	40	42	43	41
II	47	44	51	38
III	42	40	44	44

Solution: Let us take hypothesis that there is no significant difference in the treatment and plots of land. Applying analysis of variance techniques. (40 assumed)

Plot	*A*	*B*	*C*	*D*	*Total*
I	0	+2	+3	+1	+6
II	+7	+4	+11	-2	+20
III	+2	0	+4	+4	+10
	+9	+6	+18	+3	+36

$$\text{Correction factor} = \frac{T^2}{N} = \frac{36^2}{12} = \frac{1296}{12} = 108$$

Sum of squares between treatments

$$= \frac{9^2}{3} + \frac{6^2}{3} + \frac{18^2}{3} + \frac{3^2}{3}$$

$$= \frac{81}{3} + \frac{36}{3} + \frac{324}{3} + \frac{9}{3} - \frac{T^2}{N}$$

$= 27 + 12 + 108 + 3 = 150 - 108 =$ **42**

Sum of squares between plots of land

$$= \frac{6^2}{4} + \frac{20^2}{4} + \frac{10^2}{4} - \frac{T^2}{N}$$

$$= \frac{36}{4} + \frac{400}{4} + \frac{100}{4} - \frac{T^2}{N}$$

$= 9 + 100 + 25 - 108$

$= 134 - 108 =$ **26**

$v = N - 1 = 3 - 1 = 2$

Total sum of squares

$$= 0^2 + 7^2 + 2^2 + 2^2 + 4^2 + 0^2 + 3^2 + 11^2 + 4^2 + 1^2 + -2^2 + 4^2 + 6^2 + 20^2 + 10^2 - \frac{T^2}{N}$$

$$= 0 + 49 + 4 + 4 + 16 + 0 + 9 + 121 + 16 + 1 + 4 + 16 + 36 + 400 + 100$$

$$= 776 - 108 = \mathbf{668}$$

ANOVA TABLE

	SS		MS		F
Between columns	42	4 – 1 = 3	14	42 ÷ 3	$\frac{14}{300} = 0.04$
Between rows	26	3 – 1 = 2	13	$\frac{26}{2}$	$\frac{13}{300} = 0.04$
Residual	600	5	300		
Total	668	11			

The calculated value of F is less than the table value the hypothesis is accepted.

Non-parametric test: Non-parametric is a collection of tool for data analysis. It is simple to understand and easy to apply. They do not require lengthy and laborious computations. They are applicable to all types of data. It is useful to study the pilot study. If we apply a test to the hypothesis without a modal, it is known as **"distribution free test" or the Non-parametric test.** Non-parametric tests do not make an assumption about the parameters of the population. They do not make use of the parameters of the distribution. Non-parametric tests are used in practice and presented in below for discussion.

(a) Sign Tests
(b) Fisher Irwin Test
(c) Mc-Newer Test
(d) Signed Rank Test
(e) Rank Sum Test
(f) One Sample Runs Test
(g) Spearman's Rank Correlation
(h) Kendall's Coefficient of Concordance

(a) Sign test is one of the non-parametric tests. It is easy to understand. It is based on the direction of + or – signs of observations in a sample. The sign test may be classified as **one sample and two sample sign test**. One sample sign test is very simple. It test the null hypothesis. Two sample sign test is useful in computation of paired data.

Illustration 28: A typing institute provides 6 months intensive programme. It provides training programme to the students on an average at least 60 words per minute. A random sample of 20 participants in a typing test and the median number of words per minute. Test the hypothesis that the median typing speed of the students.

Students	A	B	C	D	E	F	G	H	I	J	K	L	M	N	O
Words per minute	80	75	52	70	65	58	87	72	79	65	57	69	59	55	54

Solution: The experimental procedure.

Population Median = 60. Level of significance 5%. Calculation of number of sign.

Students	*Word per minute*	*WPM 60d*
A	80	+20
B	75	+15
C	52	–8
D	70	+10
E	65	+05
F	58	–02
G	87	+17
H	72	+12
I	79	+19
J	65	+5
K	67	+7
L	69	+9
M	59	–1
N	55	–5
O	54	–6
No. of + signs	10	
No. of – signs	05	
	15	

$$K = \frac{N-1}{2} - (0.98)\sqrt{n} \qquad n = 15$$

$$K = \frac{(15-1)}{2} - (0.98)\sqrt{15}$$

$$K = \frac{14}{2} - (0.98)(3.87)$$

$$= 7 - 3.79 = 3.21$$

Since the alternate hypothesis is one sided, we obtain the probability 0.05 since S > K the null hypothesis is accepted.

Illustration 29: Hindusthan Lever Limited framed a new credit policy regarding the collection of account receivables. The particulars are provided before and after new collection policy. Use the 0.05 significance level.

Before	32	30	36	37	42	44	35	40	36	47	30	29	27	43	38
After	34	31	35	34	39	45	42	43	39	46	29	35	32	40	38

Solution: Calculation of signs + and – would be as follows

Before new credit policy

Before (1st) **(1)**	*After (credit new)* **(2)**	*Derivation* **1-2 = 3**
32	34	–
30	31	–
36	35	+
37	34	+
42	39	+
44	45	–
35	42	–
40	43	–
36	39	–
47	46	+
30	29	+
29	35	–
27	32	–
43	40	+
38	38	0

$$K = \frac{n-1}{2} - (0.98)\sqrt{N}$$

$$K = \frac{14-1}{2} - (0.98)\sqrt{14}$$

$$K = \frac{13}{2} - (0.98)(3.74)$$

$$K = 6.5 - 3.66 = 2.84$$

Since S > K the null hypothesis is accepted, there is no significance in new credit policy of the company.

(b) Fisher Irwin Test: Fisher Irwin test is another important test in non-parametric test. It is a distribution free test used in testing a hypothesis. It is used for testing a new tool applied by a unit. A business concern may design a new programme of training to compare with old training system. The impact of new training programme can be measured through this system. It is useful to study the worker's performance.

(c) McNewer Test: McNewer test is another important test in non-parametric test. It is used to calculate for two related samples. It is specially useful before and after measurement of the same subject. According to this method the subject is divided into equal groups as favourable and unfavourable views. It also categorised as favourable and unfavourable things. It tries to judge the significance of any observed change in view of the same subject before and after treatment. The following problem will reveal the situation.

Illustration 30: From the following information, test at 5% level of significance. Information collected from 1200 respondents is presented

Before treatment	*After treatment*	
	Unfavourable response	*Favourable response*
Favourable response	250	350
Unfavourable response	450	150

Solution: Let us take a null hypothesis that there has been no change in the people's attitude before and after the experiment.

$H_0 = P(A) = P(D)$
$H_0 = P(A) \neq P(D)$

$$x^2 = \frac{(|A - D| - 1)^2}{A + D} = \frac{(1250 - 1501 - 1)^2}{250 + 150}$$

$$= \frac{100 \times 100}{400} = \frac{10000}{400} = 25$$

Degree of freedom = 1

From the chi-square distribution table the value of x^2 for 1 degree of freedom at 5 per cent level of significance is 3.84. The calculated value of x^2 is 25. The calculated value is greater than the table value. Hence we should reject the null hypothesis. Therefore the change in people's attitude before and after the experiment is significant.

(d) Signed Rank Test: Signed rank test is also known as **Wilcoxon matched test**. In this method the difference between pairs will be observed. It can be used to judge the pairs performance.

Illustration 31: The following information is related to brands of different companies. The following data is provided. Test the hypothesis using Wilcoxon matched pair test.

Pair	*Brand x*	*Brand y*
1	76	54
2	46	44
3	50	46
4	56	44
5	61	50
6	50	35
7	55	27
8	61	61
9	41	46
10	64	56
11	59	55
12	59	60
13	37	47
14	58	60
15	68	43

Test the hypothesis at 5 per cent level of significance level.

Solution: Let us take the null hypothesis that there is no difference between the perceived quality of two samples. We should also take up alternative hypothesis that these will be difference between the perceived quality of two samples.

Pair	*Brand x*	*Brand y*	*Difference*	*Rank*	*Rank with signs*	
					+	–
1	76	54	22	13	13	
2	46	44	02	2.5	2.5	
3	50	46	04	4.5	4.5	
4	56	44	12	11	11	
5	61	50	11	10	10	
6	50	35	15	12	12	
7	55	27	28	15	15	
8	61	61	0	–	–	–
9	41	46	–5	6	–	–6
10	64	56	8	7	7	–
11	59	55	4	4.5	4.5	–
12	59	60	–1	1	–	–1
13	37	47	–10	9		–9
14	58	60	–2	2.5		–2.5
15	68	43	25	14	14	
					93.5	–18.5

n = 15 – 1 = 14 T = – 18.5

5% level of significance is 25

The calculated value of T is 18.5, which is less than the table value of 25. Hence we reject the null hypothesis. Therefore, there is difference between the perceived quality of the two samples.

(e) Rank Sum Test: Rank sum tests are consists with two kinds of tests. They are (a) U test, (b) H test. These two tests are known as Wilcoxon-Mann Whitney Test. It is related to pairs of samples.

"U" Test: "U" test is also known as Wilcoxon-Mann-Whitney test. It is a popular test amongst the rank sum tests. It is used to determine whether two independent samples have been drawn from the same population. It applies under general conditions and requires only that the populations sampled are continuous. It can be computed by the following formula:

$$U = n_1 n_2 + \frac{n_1(n_1 + 1)}{2} - R_1$$

Illustration 32: From the following information calculate "U" test. Two samples are provided for testing at 10% level of significance. The values in one sample are 55, 40, 71, 59, 48, 41, 75, 50, 75, 76, 62 and 80. In another sample they are 46, 42, 63, 54, 34, 46, 72, 43, 70, 74, 55 and 74.

Solution:

Size of sample item in ascending order	*Rank*	*Name of related sample*
34	1	B
40	2	A
41	3	A
42	4	B
43	5	B
46	6.5	B
46	6.5	B
48	8	A
50	9	A
54	10	B
55	11.5	B
55	11.5	A
59	13	A
62	14	A
63	15	B
69	16	B
71	17	A
72	18	B
74	19.5	B
74	19.5	B
75	21.5	A
75	21.5	A
76	23	A
80	24	A

From the above data we must calculate R_1 and R_2 ranks.

R_1 = 2 + 3 + 8 + 9 + 11.5 + 13 + 14 + 17 + 21.5 + 21.5 + 23 + 24 = 167.5

R_2 = 1 + 4 + 5 + 6.5 + 6.5 + 10 + 11.5 + 15 + 16 + 18 + 19.5 + 19.5 = 132.5

n_1 = 12 $n_2 = 12$

$$U = n_1 n_2 + \frac{n_1(n_1+1)}{2} - R$$

$$U = 12 \times 12 + \frac{12(12+1)}{2} - 167.5$$

$$U = 144 + \frac{12 \times 13}{2} - 167.5$$

$$U = 144 + \frac{156}{2} - 167.5$$

$$U = 144 + 78 - 167.5 = 54.5$$

$$U = 54.5$$

$$\mu_\mu = \frac{n_1 \times n_2}{2} = \frac{(12)(12)}{2} = \frac{144}{2} = 72$$

$$\sigma_\mu = \sqrt{\frac{12 \times 12(12+12+1)}{12}}$$

$$\sigma_\mu = \sqrt{\frac{144(25)}{12}}$$

$$\sigma_\mu = \sqrt{\frac{3600}{12}} = \sqrt{300} = 17.32$$

Upper limit $= \mu_\mu + 1.64\ \sigma_\mu$
$= 72 + 1.64\ (17.32)$
$= 72 + 28.40 = 100.40$

Lower limit $= \mu_o + 1.64\ \sigma_o$
$= 72 - 1.64\ (17.32)$
$= 72 - 28.40 - 43.60$

The observed value of U is 54.5, it will be in acceptance the null hypothesis can be accepted. The two samples come from identical population at 10% level.

In the same way we calculate "U" test with R_2

$$U = n_1 n_2 + \frac{n_2(n_2+1)}{2} - R_2$$

$$= (12)(12) + \frac{12(12+1)}{2} - 132.5$$
$$= 144 + \frac{12(13)}{2} - 132.5$$
$$= 144 + 78 - 132.5$$
$$= 222 - 132.5 = 89.5$$

It will be accepted. Conclusion remains the same.

"H" Test: "H" test is also called as Kruskal Wallis test. It is used to test the null hypothesis. It does not require the assumption. It can be computed as follows:

$$H = \frac{12}{n(n+1)} \sum_{i=1}^{K} \frac{R_i^2}{ni} - 3(n+1)$$

Illustration 33: From the following information is related to cricket match score. Use Kruskal-Wallis Test at 5% level of significance to test the hypothesis. Bowling result as follows

With ball No. A	273, 284, 259, 250, 264
With ball No. B	254, 277, 304, 270, 278
With ball No. C	262, 257, 241, 248, 268
With ball No. D	281, 244, 299, 272, 270

Solution:

Bowling results	*Rank*	*Name of the ball*
304	1	B
299	2	D
284	3	A
281	4	D
278	5	B
277	6	B
273	7	A
272	8	D
270	9	B

(Contd.)

(Contd.)

Bowling results	*Rank*	*Name of the ball*
268	10	C
264	11	A
262	12	C
260	13	D
259	14	A
257	15	C
254	16	B
250	17	A
248	18	C
244	19	D
241	20	C

Ball A	*Rank*	*Ball B*	*Rank*	*Ball C*	*Rank*	*Ball D*	*Rank*
273	7	254	16	262	12	281	4
284	3	277	6	257	15	244	19
259	14	304	1	241	20	299	2
250	17	270	9	248	18	272	8
264	11	278	5	268	10	270	13
$n_1 = 5$	$R_1 = 52$	$n_2 = 5$	$R_2 = 37$	$n_3 = 5$	$R_3 = 75$	$n_4 = 5$	$R_4 = 46$

$$n = 20$$

$$H = \frac{12}{20(20+1)}\left[\frac{52^2}{5} + \frac{37^2}{5} + \frac{75^2}{5} + \frac{46^2}{5}\right] - 3(20+1)$$

$$= (0.02857)\,(2362.8) - 63$$

$$= 67.51 - 63 = 4.51$$

The table value of x^2 is 7.815. The calculated value is less than table value. We accept null hypothesis.

(f) One Sample Run Test: One sample test is related to judge the randomness of a sample of a observed data. Conducting a survey is a part of statistical investigation. This test will be calculated with the following formula:

$$\mu_\mu = \frac{2n_1n_2}{n_1 + n_2} + 1$$

$$\sigma_r = \sqrt{2n_1n_2 \frac{(2n_1n_2 - n_1 - n_2)}{(n_1 + n_2)^2(n_1 + n_2 - 1)}}$$

(g) Spearman's Rank Correlation: Spearman's rank correlation was developed by famous statistician Charles Spearman in 1900. It is related to find out the correlation of that exists between the two sets of ranks. It is a measure of tool that is based on the ranks of the observation. It can be computed by the following formula:

$$r = 1 - \left(\frac{6\varepsilon d^2}{n(n^2 - 1)}\right)$$

$$\sigma_r = \frac{1}{\sqrt{n-1}}$$

(h) Kendall's Coefficient of Concordance: Kendall's coefficient of concordance is an important test in non-parametric test. It is used for determining the degree of association among several sets of ranking objects. It is represented by W.

Illustration 34: The following information is related to a song competition.

	Individuals						
	A	B	C	D	E	F	G
Judge 1	2	4	3	1	5	7	6
Judge 2	3	7	2	4	6	5	1
Judge 3	7	5	4	3	1	6	2
Judge 4	6	4	3	5	7	1	2

Is there any significant agreement in ranking assigned by Judges? Test at 5% level of significance.

Solution: First we must develop matrix as follows:

$$W = \frac{S}{\frac{1}{12}K^2(n^3 - n)}$$

$$\bar{R}_j = \frac{\varepsilon R_i}{N}$$

	Individuals							
	A	B	C	D	E	F	G	
Judge 1	2	4	3	1	5	7	6	
Judge 2	3	7	2	4	6	5	1	
Judge 3	7	5	4	3	1	6	2	
Judge 4	6	4	3	5	7	1	2	
Total of rank	18	20	12	13	19	19	11	= 112
$R_1 - \bar{R}_i$	4	16	64	9	9	9	25	= 136

$$\bar{R}_i = \frac{112}{7} = 16 \qquad S = 136$$

$$W = \frac{136}{\frac{1}{12}(4)^2(7^3 - 7)}$$

$$W = \frac{136}{\frac{16}{12} \times (343 - 7)}$$

$$W = \frac{136}{1.33 \times (336)}$$

$$w = \frac{136}{446.88} = 0.30$$

The table value of W, at 5% level of significance is 217.0. The calculated value is 0.30, hence we reject the null hypothesis.

INDEX

"A" test, 144
Absolute experiment, 45
Accuracy, 43, 113-14, 146-47
Ad hoc basis, 84
Alternative hypothesis, 157-58
Analysis of variance (ANOVA), 126, 191, 200
Analytical research study, 6
Applied and Fundamental Research Study, 7
Arbitrary
approach, 84
scales, 88-89
Area sampling method, 21-22
Attitude scale, 88
Audiometer, 112

Bain and Co., 118
Basic concepts in research design, 43
Basic research, 7
Bayesian theory, 147
Biased errors, 69
Bi-modal, 129
Bi-variate analysis, 125
Bi-variate population, 133-34

C.R. Rao table, 64
Canonical analysis, 126
Case study, 116-17
Casual analysis, 126
Categorical and comparative, 82
Cellular services, 9, 102
Census
inquiry, 20, 57
method, 67-68, 138
Central editing, 124
Central tendency
error of, 87
measures of, 127
Chance sampling, 21, 62
Chi-square test, 28, 74, 142, 159, 191
Classification, 120-22, 137
Clinical interview, 100
Cluster sampling method, 22, 65, 66
Coding, 27, 123-24, 137
Coefficient of
colligation, 136
contingency, 135, 136
correlation, 160
Collection of data, 4, 15-16, 21, 24, 41, 46, 48-49, 58, 60-61, 70, 94-95, 114-15, 120, 139, 147
Comparative
experiment, 45
scale, 87
Completely randomised design, 54
Complex factorial design, 56
Complex sample designing method, 21, 23
Composite index, 136
Conceptual research, 8
Consensus scale, 89
Construction techniques, 88
Consumer pulse, 12
Content analysis, 110
Contingency table, 74
Continuous and non-continuous variable, 44
Control group, 45, 54
Convenience sampling, 22
Copal Parthers, 118
Correlated pairs, 144
Correlation, 6, 45, 75, 84, 126-27, 131, 133-34, 141, 144, 160-62, 164, 166, 182-84, 201, 211
analysis, 126
measures of, 74
Council of Scientific and Industrial Research, 5
Criteria validity, 79
Cross tabulation, 134
Cumulative scales, 89, 91

Data processing, 123
Decision oriented research, 9
Deliberate sampling method, 21-22
Dependent and independent, 44
Depth interviews, 7, 11, 107, 112, 117
Descriptive and analytical research study, 6
Descriptive studies, 99
Diagnosis, 20, 117
Differential scales, 89
Digital economy, 11
Direct and indirect taxation system, 13
Direct personal investigation, 99
Disguised observation, 98
Dispersion, 127, 130-31, 137
Distribution free test, 201, 204
Dolls Play test, 109

Econometrics, 5
Editing, 27, 123-24, 137
E-mails, 102
Empirical and conceptual research study, 8
Error variance, 140

Errors hallo effect, 87
Estimation, 142, 145
E-test, 75
Evalue Serve, 118-19
Exit polls, 7
Expected frequencies method, 135
Experience survey, 37, 43, 46-47
Experiment, 20, 24, 45, 52, 72, 96
Experimental approach, 10
Experimental designs, kinds of, 51
Experimental hypothesis testing research, 45
Experimental study, 50
Experimental type of research, 8
Experimental units, 45
Experimentation, 20
Exploration, 19
Exploratory research, 9, 46, 98
Extraneous variable, 44, 54-55
Eye cameras, 112

Factor scales, 85, 89, 93
Factorial design, 54, 56
Fast food culture, 22
Field
  editing, 124
  research, 15
Fisher Irwin Test, 201, 204
Fisher, R.A., 50, 53, 160
Flexibility, 80
Focused interview, 100
Forecasting business cycles, 132
Formal
  design, 20
  experimental design, 52-53
Frederic Le play, 116
F-test, 28, 75, 141, 158, 191, 200
Functional relationship, 126
Fundamental research, 6-8, 32

Genpact, 118
Geometric Mean, 128, 130
Gosset, W.S., 141
Graphic rating scale, 86

Harmonic Mean, 128, 130
Historical research, 9
Holtzman Inkblot test, 109-10
Homogeneity, 142
H-Test, 212
Hypothesis, 5, 18-19, 22, 28, 38, 44, 46, 50, 137, 156-57, 159
  designing of a, 157
  procedure for testing, 157
  testing of, 17, 28, 142-43, 159
  testing research, 5, 45

Independence of error, 142
Independent variable, 44
Index numbers, 136-37
Indian Council of Agricultural Research, 5
Indian Council of Social Science Research, 5, 32, 115
Indian Institute of Science, 5, 32
Indian Statistical Institute, 5, 32
Indirect interviewing technique, 107
Indirect oral examination, 99
Indisproportional method, 65
Inferential
  analysis, 126
  statistics, 127
Informal
  design, 20
  experimental design, 52
Insight analysis, 47
Inter-correlation basis, 84
Interpretation, 8, 17, 19, 28
Interval
  estimate, 142
  scale form, 76, 83
Interviews, 11, 22, 76, 99, 102, 105, 112-13, 117, 118
Itemised rating scale, 85, 86

Judgement sampling, 21-22

Karl Pearson's correlation, 134
Kendall's Coefficient of Concordance, 212
KPO, 118-19

Laboratory research, 15
Latin square design, 54-55
Leniency, error of, 87
Library research process, 15
Linear correlation, 134
Local control, 51
Longitudinal research, 8
Lorenz curve, 131-32
Lottery system, 21, 62
Louis Gutman analysis, 91

Market
  analysis, 12
  research, 12, 118
McKinsey & Co., 118
McNewer test, 204
Mean, 15, 75, 128-32, 140, 141, 144-50, 157, 159-60, 165-69, 176-78, 184, 196-97, 199
  deviation, 131-32
Measurement scales in research operations, 74

Median, 15, 75, 89, 128, 132, 160, 202
Miscellanceous factors, 147
Miscellaneous research study, 8
Mixed sampling, 23
Mode, 15, 20, 79, 128-29, 130, 132, 160
Motion picture cameras, 112
Motivation research, 7, 12
Multidimensional scaling, 93
Multimedia Message Services (MMS), 102
Multiple correlation, 134
Multiple discriminant analysis, 126
Multiple factors orientation, 83
Multiple regression, 126, 135, 137
Multi-stage sampling method, 21, 23
Multi-variate
    analysis, 125-26, 137
    population, 133, 135

Negative correlation, 134
Non-continuous variables, 44
Non-directive interview, 100
Non-parametric test, 75, 159, 201
Non-participant observation, 98
Non-probability samples, 21-22, 62
Non-sampling errors, 69-71
Non-structured study, 103
Normality, 142
Null hypothesis, 157, 158
Numerical
    information, 10, 125
    scale, 86

Observation design, 24, 41-42, 96-98
Observation or interview method, 96
Office Tiger, 118-19
One sample run test, 210
Open sky policy, 10
Operations research, 9, 12
Opinion research, 7
Opinionnaire, 88, 93
Ordinal data, 73
Osgood, Charles, 93

Paired comparison, 87
Parameter, 140, 143, 157
Parametric tests, 74, 159, 191, 199, 201-02
Partial correlation, 134-35, 144, 165
Participant observation, 97-98
Pearson, Karl, 142
Personal interview, 15, 22, 24-25, 98-101, 105, 115
Personal preference orientation, 82
Pictorial technique, 109
Pilot survey, 36, 106
Pipal research, 118-19
Popular personalities, 109, 113
Population mean, estimating, 145
Population proportion, estimating, 145-46
Positive correlation, 134
Practicality, test of, 78-79
Probability, 21, 23, 62, 141, 143, 152-53, 156, 158, 203
    sampling, 21, 23, 62
Projective techniques, 107
Proportion, 135, 141, 150
Psychogalvanometer, 112
Pulse of consumers, 16
Pupilometric camera, 112
Puzzles, 108-09

Qualitative analysis, 110, 116
Qualitative approach, 10-11
Qualitative research, 7
Quantitative approach, 10
Quantitative classification, 122
Quartile range, 132
Quasi-random sampling method, 65
Questionnaire, 26, 48, 61, 70, 77, 80-81, 90, 102-06, 115, 117-18, 124
Quota sampling method, 21, 23

Rand Corporation table, 64
Random replication design, 54-55
Random sampling, 21, 23, 51, 62, 64-65
Randomisation, 50-51
Randomised block design, 54-55
Range, 131
Rank
    order, 87-88
    sum test, 201, 206
Ranking scale, 82, 87
Rating scale, 85-86
Ratio scale, 75-76
Reciprocal relationship, 134
Regression analysis, 126, 131
Reliability, test of, 78-79
Replication, 50-51, 55
    principle of, 51, 54
Research
    approaches, 9
    design, 17, 19, 41, 42-43, 46-47
    engine, 118
    importance of, 11
    method, 3, 14-15, 56
    methodology, 3, 14-15
    process, 16
Response analysis, 92
Restricted sampling method, 64
Root square deviation, 132

Rorschach test, 109-10
Rosenzweig test, 109-10

Sales forecasting and business budgeting, 12
Sample design, 21, 23, 58, 61-62, 140
  kinds of, 62
Sample survey, 58, 67, 71, 96
Sampling
  advantages and disadvantages of, 67
  design, 21, 57, 60, 62
  error, 24, 61, 68-71, 140-41
  fundamentals of, 138
  method, 21-23, 42, 49, 64, 68-70, 117, 139
  of attributes, 143
  of variables, 143-44
  plan, precision of, 62
  process of, 58, 60
  process, 139-40
  statistics, 127, 129
  technique, 58, 66, -68
  theory, 142-43
Sandler, Joseph, 144
Scale properties, 83
Scaling, 72, 81, 83-84
Scalogram analysis, 92
Schedules method, 24-25, 96
Scientific
  method, 16
  differential, 93
Sentence completion tests, 108
Short Message Services (SMS), 102
Sign test, 202
Signed rank test, 201, 205
Simple arithmetic mean, 128
Simple correlation, 134, 137
Simple factorial design, 56
Simple random sampling method, 21
Simulation approach, 11
Skewness, 127, 133, 137
Smith, Babington, 63-64
Social microscope, 116
Social science sector, 11, 14
Sociometry, 108-09
Spearman, Charles, 211
Spearman's rank correlation, 134, 212
Special purpose survey, 24
Spencer, Herbert, 116
Standard deviation, 15, 75, 131-33, 140, 144, 146-49, 166-69, 176, 184
Standard error, 144
Statistical
  average, 127, 130
  design, 41-42
  estimation, 142
  inference, 142-43, 156
  inferences, 27, 142
  techniques, 15
  tools, 126
Story test, 108
Strata, 23, 65
Stratified sampling, 21, 23, 64-65
Structured observation, 97
Study reports, 117
Suci, G.J., 93
Summated scales, 89-90
Systematic bias, 61
Systematic sampling method, 21-22, 65

Tabulation, 27, 122-23, 137
  principles of, 123
Tannebum, P.H., 93
Techniques involved in research problem, 35
Telecommunication sector, 10
Telephone interview method, 24-25, 101
Thematic apperception test, 109
Thurstons, L.L., 88-89
Tippets random numbers, 63
Tomkins-Horn picture test, 110
"t" table, 141
T-Test, 28, 141, 165

Unclear response, 125
Undimensional analysis, 125
Univariate
  index, 136
  population, 133
University Degree, 28
Unrestricted sampling method, 64
Unstructured interviews, 99
Unweighted indices, 137
"U" Test, 212

Validity, test of, 78
Variance ratio test, 141
Variation, 54, 63, 65, 126, 131, 197
Verbal tests, 110

Warranty cards, 107
Weighted arithmetic mean, 128, 129
Weighted indices, 137
Wilcoxon matched test, 205
Wilcoxon-Mann Whitney test, 206
WNS knowledge, 118
Word power, 108

Yule's coefficient of association, 136

Z test, 159, 164